ANATOMY OF FITNESS 501

Yoga Exercises

hinkler

Published by Hinkler Books Pty Ltd 2018
45–55 Fairchild Street
Heatherton Victoria 3202 Australia
www.hinkler.com

hinkler

Created by Moseley Road Inc.
Cover Designer: Sam Grimmer
Prepress: Splitting Image
Production Director: Adam Moore
Designer: Philippa Baile www.oiloften.co.uk
Photographer: Naila Ruechel
Author: Nancy J. Hajeski

ISBN: 978 1 4889 3406 3

Printed and bound in China

GENERAL DISCLAIMER

The contents of this book are intended to provide useful information to the general public. All materials, including texts, graphics, and images, are for informational purposes only and are not a substitute for medical diagnosis, advice, or treatment for specific medical conditions. All readers should seek expert medical care and consult their own physicians before commencing any exercise program or for any general or specific health issues. The author and publishers do not recommend or endorse specific treatments, procedures, advice, or other information found in this book and specifically disclaim all responsibility for any and all liability, loss, or risk, personal or otherwise, which is incurred as a consequence, directly or indirectly, of the use or application of any of the material in this publication.

ANATOMY OF FITNESS™

501

Yoga Exercises

Craft perfect workouts for your own training goals
and discover the amazing hidden structure of your body

Contents

Introduction

Yoga is a physical, spiritual, and mental discipline rooted in simplicity. You assume a pose, hold it, and then flow it into another pose. There is no heavy lifting of equipment, no quick or jerking movements, no endless repetition of sets. It is a study in economy of motion and restrained grace. There are basic and intermediate poses that can be achieved with relative ease, and advanced poses that are quite intricate and can take years to master. Yet even the simplest pose requires control, concentration, and alignment. Many intermediate and advanced poses also require strength and flexibility, plus a good sense of balance. You will acquire these attributes—control, focus, strength, balance, and flexibility—in increasing measure as you deepen your commitment to yoga and increase the complexity of your poses.

Yoga also offers mental and spiritual benefits. In Hinduism, Brahminism, and Jainism, the term yoga means "spiritual discipline," and so it represents much more than a mere exercise regimen—it is meant to alter our lives for the better. The psychological and spiritual enrichment offered by yoga was originally its chief intent. According to Georg Feuerstein, a German Indologist and author who specialized in yoga, it was meant to "bring about a profound transformation in the person based on the transcendence of the ego." This alchemy begins to take place when participants focus on proper breathing methods and on when to move large and small muscles. A quieting of the mind occurs, and the process of concentrating on the placement of a body part requires us to be wholly in the present moment. The body then becomes the conduit to something larger, deeper, and more resonant than our own narrow world.

Ideally, after an extended yoga session, you should feel refreshed, refocused, and energized—and yet oddly tranquil.

A brief history

The precise origins of yoga are open to debate. What is known is that yoga was first developed by the Indus-Saravati culture of northern India more than 5,000 years ago. Yoga was first mentioned in the Rig Veda—the oldest of the ancient spiritual texts of India comprised of a collection of songs, mantras, and rituals—in reference to the concept of discipline. Yoga was originally meant to foster a greater understanding of the world; it then evolved into a study of the self, with self-enlightenment the ultimate goal. The collection of Hindu texts called the Upanishads set out this path as "studying under a teacher and dedicated one's life to the practice of yoga." It was around the 6th century BC that the poses and meditation became important elements of yoga, and these were in large part implemented by the teachings of the Buddha.

Modern yoga

Yoga was first introduced to educated Westerners in the middle of the 19th century along with other aspects of Indian philosophy. In the 1890s, the acclaimed yogi Swami Vivekananda toured Europe and the United States. His popularity was bolstered by many intellectuals, including the Transcendentalists, whose numbers once included Ralph Waldo Emerson and Henry David Thoreau, and who had themselves been

inspired by German Romanticism and the interest of philosophers such as Georg Hegel and Arthur Schopenhauer in Indian culture and ideologies. The Theosophists also influenced the American view and acceptance of yoga. This movement embraced a collection of mystical and occult philosophies; its adherents believed that the ancient knowledge of the past could offer an understanding of the natural world and lead to enlightenment and even salvation.

During the early 20th century in India, many ancient customs continued to be discouraged by the British, and few Indians continued to practice yoga. But a young man named Tirumalai Krishnamacharya had been exposed to yoga as a child, and when a revival of Indian traditions occurred during his formative years, he was able to study Hindu ritual, Indian law, Sanskrit, and the Ayurveda, Indian medicine. But his first allegiance was to yoga, and it was he who more or less created what we consider the modern, more physical style of yoga—Ashtanga Vinyasa yoga. This was partially a result of the patronage of the Maharajah of Mysore, a diabetic who was interested in the potential healing powers of the discipline. Kirshnamacharya believed that yoga should follow three stages: during youth we develop muscular strength and flexibility; during our adult "family" years we maintain our health; and lastly we focus on our spirituality. Krishnamacharya was also the first yogi to allow females to study—he taught Indira Devi, the world's first female yoga teacher. Another influential proponent was Swami Sivananda, who maintained that modern yoga was comprised of five principles: proper relaxation, proper exercise, proper breathing, proper diet, and positive thinking and meditation.

By the 1960s, yoga had become linked with the youthful counterculture movement and with the hippies, with their interest in meditation and Eastern

spirituality. The fitness and health-club craze of the 1980s further heightened interest in yoga, and it was not long before aspirants of every age and economic background were practicing their Downward Facing Dog and "getting in touch with their inner guru."

The yoga tradition

The yoga practiced today by Westerners places a greater emphasis on the body than the earlier versions. Many people are now drawn to yoga as a means to get in shape, slim down, overcome a sedentary lifestyle, or stretch muscles made tight by stress or daily pressures. Yet the traditions of classical yoga remain—the poses, or asanas, are still called by their melodic Sanskrit names—Ananda Balasana, Savasana, and Bhujangasana, and the foundation poses—like the Crow, Camel, and Locust—are still revered as they were a hundred years ago. And regardless of where you practice, in your own home, at the Y, or in a dedicated yoga studio, you are part of an ongoing tradition that is thousands of years old.

The top disciplines

Over time, several distinct types of yoga have evolved. Vinyana is a fast-paced version that links breathing and movement; it is often practiced with music. Hatha is a gentle, slow-paced version that is great for beginners. Iyengar improves alignment and form and is good for those recovering from injuries. Ashtanga is ideal for overachievers—it focuses on repeated routines and strict guidelines. Bikrim consists of 26 poses and two breathing exercises practiced in a heated room. Kundalini, best for those who want a spiritual connection, incorporates repetitive exercises and breathing work with singing, chanting, and meditating. There is also Yin yoga, where poses are held for minutes to provide a therapeutic stretch, and Restorative yoga, with longer holds for deep relaxation.

Yoga for healing

In recent years, yoga has also been studied as a possible complementary intervention for treating cancer, heart disease, asthma, and schizophrenia, among other ailments. Although the research on cancer provided inconclusive results, the studies on the other conditions indicated that yoga may be effective for reducing risk factors and aiding in the patient's psychological healing process.

Inside this book

This book is meant to introduce you to a number of foundational yoga poses and their many variations. The chapters are based on body positions, such as standing, reclining, bending forward, and sitting. Within these chapters are a series of featured foundation poses, each offering a brief introduction, bulleted steps to follow, one or more photos of the pose, and tips on the correct way to approach the pose as well as pitfalls to avoid. These featured poses also include an anatomical cutaway illustration showing the areas of the body and the muscles the pose benefits. Each foundation pose is then followed by a number of related poses, with a brief description and photo of the completed pose.

By following the instructions and using the photographs as guidelines, beginners should be able to work their way from starter poses to more demanding ones. More advanced practitioners will be able to attempt variations of the poses they have already mastered, including those that may tax their strength, balance, and flexibility. Anyone who is guided by this book should come away with a sense of accomplishment, a feeling of wellness and well-being, and a noticeable level of calmness.

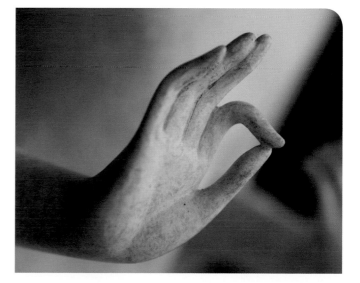

Full-Body Anatomy

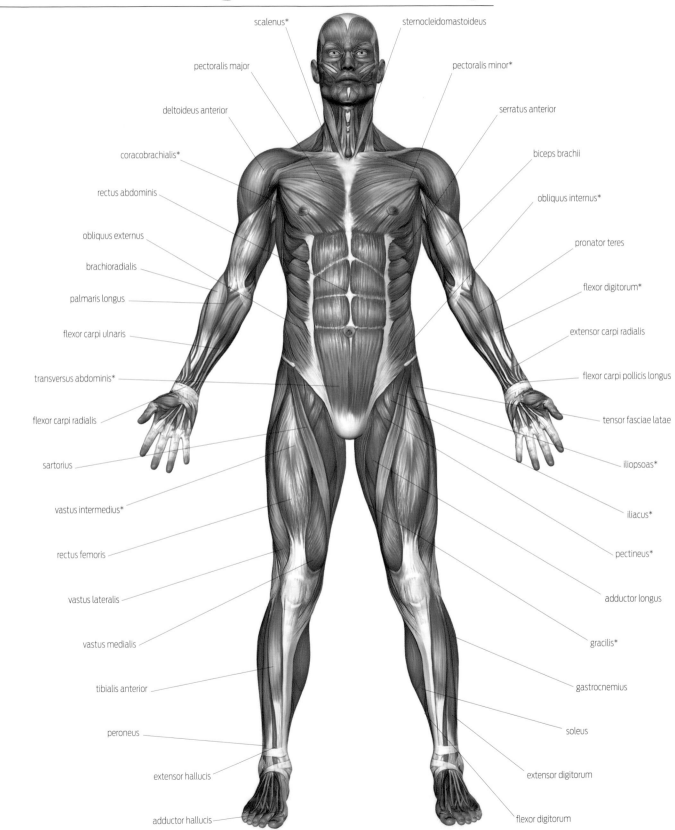

scalenus*

sternocleidomastoideus

pectoralis major

pectoralis minor*

deltoideus anterior

serratus anterior

coracobrachialis*

biceps brachii

rectus abdominis

obliquus internus*

obliquus externus

pronator teres

brachioradialis

flexor digitorum*

palmaris longus

extensor carpi radialis

flexor carpi ulnaris

transversus abdominis*

flexor carpi pollicis longus

flexor carpi radialis

tensor fasciae latae

sartorius

iliopsoas*

vastus intermedius*

iliacus*

rectus femoris

pectineus*

vastus lateralis

adductor longus

vastus medialis

gracilis*

tibialis anterior

gastrocnemius

peroneus

soleus

extensor hallucis

extensor digitorum

adductor hallucis

flexor digitorum

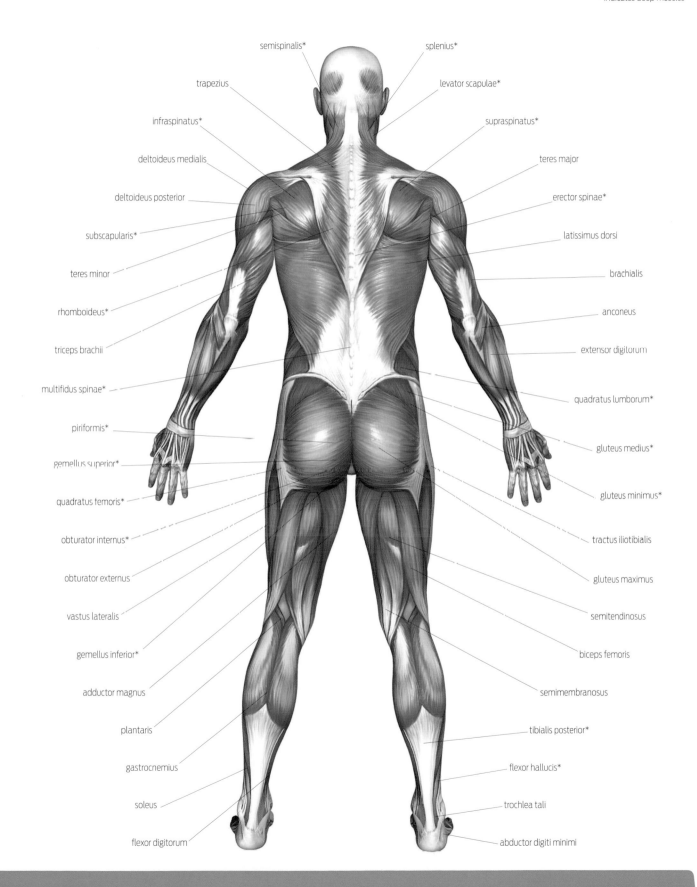

semispinalis*

splenius*

trapezius

levator scapulae*

infraspinatus*

supraspinatus*

deltoideus medialis

teres major

deltoideus posterior

erector spinae*

subscapularis*

latissimus dorsi

teres minor

brachialis

rhomboideus*

anconeus

triceps brachii

extensor digitorum

multifidus spinae*

quadratus lumborum*

piriformis*

gluteus medius*

gemellus superior*

gluteus minimus*

quadratus femoris*

tractus iliotibialis

obturator internus*

gluteus maximus

obturator externus

vastus lateralis

semitendinosus

gemellus inferior*

biceps femoris

adductor magnus

semimembranosus

plantaris

tibialis posterior*

gastrocnemius

flexor hallucis*

soleus

trochlea tali

flexor digitorum

abductor digiti minimi

11

CHAPTER ONE

Standing Poses

Standing poses are foundational to most yoga flows. Typically, these poses are practiced at the start of a workout, and therefore are the cornerstone of many fundamental movements in the practice. Standing poses create energy in the body, develop stamina, and build awareness of your body's abilities. Most standing poses require a delicate equilibrium of strength, flexibility, and balance; all of which rest on a good alignment throughout the body. Maintaining good posture and planting your feet firmly are also important qualities of a successful standing pose. Although the standing poses require a vitality that stems from the legs, the wide range of movements and variations in a standing series will engage the muscles throughout the entire body. These poses will strengthen the arms, shoulders, torso, pelvis, legs, and feet. Finding graceful balance within the standing poses will prepare you for all other asanas to follow.

001

Mountain Pose

Mountain Pose is the foundational pose from which all other standing positions and inversions follow. This pose improves spinal posture, balance and muscle alignment throughout the body. While it may seem like a basic posture, there are many subtle principles of alignment which can be applied to many of the standing poses that follow.

serratus anterior

transversus abdominis*

iliopsoas*

sartorius

vastus medialis

obliquus externus

rectus abdominis

obliquus internus*

rectus femoris

vastus lateralis

Correct form
Align yourself so that your ears, shoulders, hips, and heels are in a straight line, with your weight even across both feet.

Avoid
Avoid this pose if you are experiencing dizziness or imbalance. Always move within your range of limits and abilities.

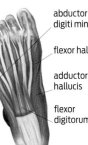

abductor digiti minimi

flexor hallucis*

adductor hallucis

flexor digitorum*

- Stand with your feet together and your arms at your sides. Press your weight evenly across the balls and arches of your feet.

- Bring your pelvis to its neutral position. Do not let your front hip bones point down or up; instead, point them straight forward. Draw your belly in slightly.

- Elongate through your torso. Exhale and release your shoulder blades away from your head, toward the back of your waist.

- Rotate your inner arms outward, bringing your hands out to your sides. Spread your fingers apart and hold your palms facing forward.

- Hold this pose for one minute, feeling your spine lengthen throughout.

002 Upward Salute

From Mountain Pose (#001), extend your arms straight up toward the ceiling. Raise your gaze upward and feel your spine and neck lengthen.

003 Reverse Prayer

From Mountain Pose (#001), extend your arms up behind your back. Press your palms together in Reverse Prayer Position. Attempt to lift your joined hands up further along your spine.

004 Hands Bound

From Mountain Pose (#001), extend your arms out behind you. Clasp your fingers together and attempt to lift your bound hands up along your spine.

005 Sideways Hands Bound

From Mountain Pose (#001), lace your fingers together and raise your arms straight above you. Keeping your fingers laced and your arms extended, drop your torso down to one side and then the other. This pose is also known as Parshva Tadasana Urdhva Baddha Hastasana, and Side Bending Pose (Parshva Bhangi).

- A Side-Bending Pose can target areas you don't often stretch and leave you feeling more balanced throughout your body.
- Side Bending Poses stretch and strengthen the muscles in the back, shoulders, and obliques, toning the stomach and waist.
- Side bends are a basic yoga preparation pose for all levels.
- Side bends prepare the spine and side waist for lateral bends and stretches required for Triangle (#029), Extended Side Angle (#074) and Half Moon (#040) Poses.

Standing Crescent

From Mountain Pose (#001), lace your fingers together and raise your arms straight above you. Keeping your fingers laced and your arms extended, lean your shoulders and chest down to one side. Keep your hips in line with your feet and ankles.

Tadasana Pose

From Mountain Pose (#001), extend your arms straight up above you. Press your palms together with your fingers pointing up to the ceiling. Shift your gaze up directly toward the ceiling.

One Leg Standing Crescent

From Mountain Pose (#001), lift one foot up from the ground. Lace your fingers together and raise your arms straight above you. Keeping your fingers laced and your arms extended, lean your shoulders and chest down to one side.

009 Shivas Vigorous Cycle of Life

To perform Tandavasana, stand straight, with fingers laced and raised above your head. Cross your left leg behind your right leg, keeping both feet flat to the ground. Lean your torso back and to the right, so you are now facing the ceiling.

- Take your time in finding the natural balance within this pose.
- Use the energy from your arms reaching upward to create length along the arching side of your body.
- Bend from your upper back to avoid putting too much pressure on the hips.
- This pose stretches the chest, abdomen, shoulders, thighs, hips, legs, and ankles.
- It provides vitality and energy throughout the body.

010
Sun Salutation Backbend

From Mountain Pose (#001), extend your arms straight up above you with your palms facing each other and your fingers pointed upward. Keeping your arms extended, drop your shoulders back into a deep backbend. This pose is also known as Surya Namaskarasana. Surya is the Sanskrit word for the sun and Namaskara derives from namas: "to bow, obeisance, reverential salutation."

· Sun Salutations build up heat in the body and are typically practiced in sequence as a warm-up routine. Always breathe through the nose when performing a Sun Salutation ritual, as this warms the air before it enters your chest, providing a meditation quality to the ritual.

· This specific Sun Salutation Pose creates space in the lower back and hip flexors. It is usually done in conjunction with a deep exhalation. With regular backbends, we can help to protect the spine by increasing mobility while strengthening the supporting muscles around the skeleton.

Menopause Relief
Mid-supine backbends can open up the chest and heart area. This can help balance blood pressure and hormonal secretion as well as relieve mood swings and hot flashes. Focusing on poses that open up the pelvic space can help avoid stress and discomfort associated with menopause.

011
Sun Salutation Bound Backbend
From Mountain Pose (#001), extend your arms straight up above you. Clasp your fingers together. Keeping your arms extended and your hands bound, drop your shoulders back into a deep backbend.

012
Chair Pose
From Mountain Pose (#001), bend your knees and lean your upper body forward so that it is at a 45-degree angle to the floor. Keep your back straight and hold for 30 seconds.

Do it Right
Perform the lowering motion with your thighs, knees, and hips alone to achieve the correct posture in your lower body. Avoid arching your back.

013

Tree Pose

Tree Pose establishes strength and balance along the leg muscles, improving one's sense of center and groundedness. This pose stretches the thighs, groins, torso, and shoulders, building strength in the ankles and calves, and toning the abdominal muscles.

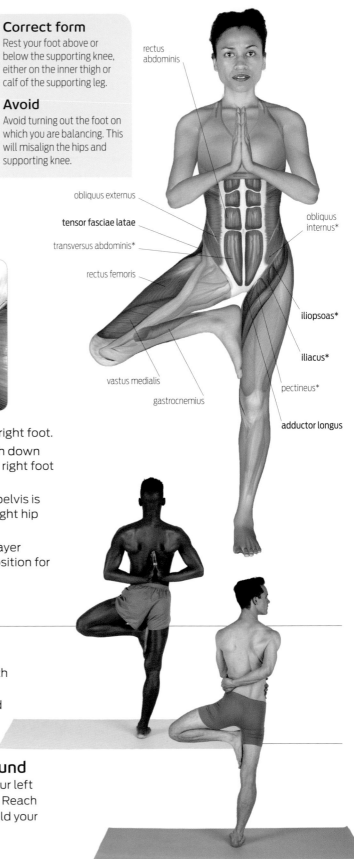

rectus abdominis

obliquus externus

tensor fasciae latae

transversus abdominis*

rectus femoris

obliquus internus*

iliopsoas*

iliacus*

pectineus*

adductor longus

vastus medialis

gastrocnemius

Annotation Key
Bold text indicates
strengthening muscles
Black text indicates
stretching muscles
* indicates deep muscles

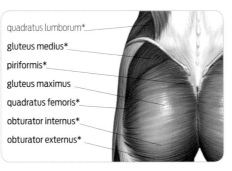

quadratus lumborum*
gluteus medius*
piriformis*
gluteus maximus
quadratus femoris*
obturator internus*
obturator externus*

- Start by standing straight, and shift your weight onto your right foot.
- Bend your right knee, lifting your foot up off the floor. Reach down and clasp your right inner ankle. Use your hand to pull your right foot alongside your inner left thigh.
- To find balance, adjust your position so the center of your pelvis is directly over your left foot. Then, adjust your hips so your right hip and left hip are aligned.
- Once you have found your balance, place your hands in Prayer Position in front of your chest. Attempt to remain in this position for 10 seconds or longer.
- Release and repeat, this time balancing on your left foot.

014 Tree Pose Reverse Prayer
Once you have found your balance, raise both hands behind your back. Press your palms together with your fingers pointed up toward the ceiling, in Reverse Prayer Position.

015 Tree Variation Revolved Half Bound
Once you have found your balance, reach your left hand across your chest to your opposite hip. Reach your right hand behind and around you to hold your left hip from behind.

016 Tree Variation Side Bending

Once balanced, extend your arms straight out to your sides. Lean your torso down to the left, so your right hand is extended up toward the ceiling.

017 Tree Variation Half Bound Upward

Once balanced, reach your hand on the same side as your raised foot behind your back and over to your opposite hip. Lift your foot off your opposite thigh, and hold your foot with your hand so your hand and foot are bound in front of your hip. Extend your free arm straight upward.

018 Hand to Foot Hand to Knee

Once balanced, reach both arms down behind you. With the hand on the same side as your raised foot, grab hold of your bent knee. Lift your foot from your thigh and grab hold of your foot with your opposite hand. Extend your raised, bent leg out behind you, keeping hold of your knee and foot with each hand.

019 Hand to Foot Hand to Knee Toppling

Once balanced, reach both arms down behind you. With the hand on the same side as your raised foot, grab hold of your bent knee. Lift your foot from your thigh and grab hold of your foot with your opposite hand. Extend your raised, bent leg out behind you, keeping hold of your knee and foot with each hand. From this position, bend forward from your hips.

Good Form

Make sure you keep the supporting foot facing forward. Turning it out will misalign your hips and supporting knee. Keep the knee facing forward.

020 Arms Raised

Once balanced in Tree Pose (#013), reach both arms straight up above you. Your palms should be facing one another and your fingers pointing straight up.

021

Extended Hand to Foot Pose

Extended Hand to Foot Pose is an important exercise in improving both balance and flexibility. When performing this pose, it is important to focus on firmly grounding the standing leg. Keep this leg straight and your spine long, before raising your other leg. Give yourself enough time to find your balance and attempt to hold the pose for 1 to 5 breaths.

Correct form
Keep your spine upright and straight with your shoulders directly in line with your hips. Keep your hips square throughout and ground the heel of your balancing leg into the floor to help you maintain balance.

Avoid
Do not let your hip tilt upward as you attempt to raise your leg. Avoid locking your knee or letting it tilt inward.

deltoideus
flexor digitorum
palmaris longus
flexor carpi radialis
flexor carpi ulnaris
pronator teres
extensor digitorum
rectus abdominis
serratus anterior
obliquus internus*
obliquus externus
gluteus maximus
vastus intermedius
vastus medialis
semimembranosus
semitendinosus
transversus abdominis*
adductor magnus
sartorius
rectus femoris
biceps femoris
vastus lateralis
soleus
tibialis anterior

iliopsoas*
iliacus*
tensor fasciae latae
pectineus*
adductor longus

Annotation Key
Bold text indicates strengthening muscles
Black text indicates stretching muscles
* indicates deep muscles

- Begin in Mountain Pose (#001). Shift your weight onto your right foot and raise your left knee. Place your right hand on your hip for balance.
- Grab onto your left big toe with your left hand—two fingers should be wrapped around the inside of your toe with your thumb around the outside.
- Rotate your right thigh slightly, and firm your supporting leg. Exhaling, extend your left leg out straight. Hold for 1 to 5 breaths before repeating on the other side.

022 Extended One Foot Pose

From Mountain Pose (#001), place both hands behind your hips. Raise one knee up to your chest. Straighten your leg out in front, in line with your hips. Point your toes.

023 Leg to Side

Begin in Extended Hand to Foot Pose (#021). On an exhale, extend your left leg straight out to your side. Hold for 1 to 5 breaths before repeating on the other side.

024 Upward Extended

Shift your weight onto your left foot and raise your right knee. Grab your right foot with both hands. Internally rotate your left thigh slightly and firm your supporting leg. Exhaling, extend your right leg straight up to your side, pulling it upward with both hands.

025 Rising Standing

Shift your weight onto your left foot and raise your right knee. Clasp your right heel with both hands. Internally rotate your left thigh slightly and firm your supporting leg. On an exhale, extend your right leg straight up, pulling it upward with both hands. Drop your torso down to the right side.

026 Hand-to-Foot Variation

From Mountain Pose (#001), place both hands firmly behind your hips for support. Raise one knee up to your chest. Once balanced, attempt to extend your leg straight out to the side. Keep your toes pointed away from you.

027 Revolved Extended

Shift your weight onto your right foot and raise your left knee. Place your left hand on your hip. Grab your left toe with your right hand. Internally rotate your right thigh slightly and firm your supporting leg. Exhaling, extend your left leg out straight across your body and to the right. Extend your left arm straight.

028 Bird of Paradise

Shift your weight onto your left foot and raise your right knee. Place your hands on your hips. Internally rotate your left thigh slightly and firm your supporting leg. Exhaling, extend your right leg out straight across your body and to the left. Move your left arm around your back and your right arm around your raised right thigh. Join your hands together around your raised leg.

029

Triangle Pose

Triangle Pose is a quintessential element of most standing yoga flows. It is known to reduce stress and increase stability. This pose lengthens the muscles on the side of the waist, while deeply extending the hamstrings and hips.

Avoid

Avoid this pose if you have low blood pressure or are experiencing headaches. Those with neck injuries or stiffness should not attempt to turn their head to the ceiling, but instead may look straight ahead or at the ground.

- Stand with your arms straight out to your sides. Step your left foot several feet back, turning it slightly outward.
- Bend your torso forward at the waist over your front leg until your torso is parallel to the ground.
- Drop your right hand to rest on your right shin.
- Turn your head upward so you are facing the ceiling. Hold this position for 30 seconds before switching sides.

Correct form

Keep your arms and legs straight throughout. Use an inhalation to lengthen your spine and an exhalation to enter the twist.

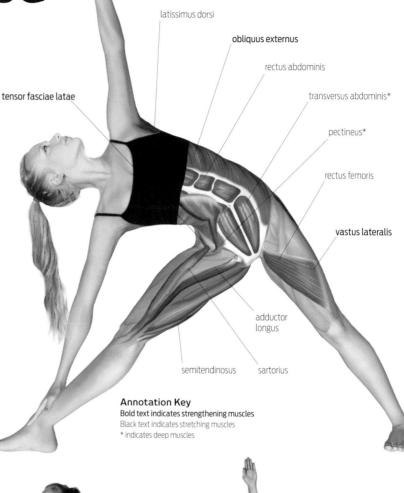

latissimus dorsi

obliquus externus

rectus abdominis

transversus abdominis*

tensor fasciae latae

pectineus*

rectus femoris

vastus lateralis

adductor longus

semitendinosus   sartorius

Annotation Key
Bold text indicates strengthening muscles
Black text indicates stretching muscles
* indicates deep muscles

030 Triangle Pose Variation

Deepen the pose by lowering your right hand all the way down to the ground, directly outside of your right foot.

031 Bound Revolved Extended Feet Spread

This is a calming twist that stretches the whole body. It helps to detoxify the digestive organs, and also soothes the mind and improves full-body coordination.

· From a start of Triangle Pose (#029), with legs spread, twist your upper torso to the right and down, so your shoulders are perpendicular to floor.

· Bend your left arm and reach out to grasp your right ankle.

· Bring your right arm across the lower back to touch your left hip. Hold for 15 to 30 seconds; reverse the direction of the twist.

Breath Control

In yoga practice, equal attention should be paid to the physical movements of the body as to the act of breathing. Your breath should guide you through your practice. Once you are able to connect your breath with your movements, and your movements with your breathing, then you will establish a moving form of meditation.

032 Revolved Triangle Pose

Spread your feet and extend both arms. Exhaling, hinge forward from your hips, twisting right. Drop your left hand on the floor by your right foot. Reach your right arm straight up.

033 Extended Side Triangle

From Triangle Pose Variation (#030), continue to fold at the waist, pulling your right arm down so it is extended parallel to the ground. This should target the muscles in your obliques.

034 Intense Side Stretch Pose Preparation

Step your left foot about 3 feet (90 cm) ahead of your right foot, with heel-to-heel alignment. On an exhale, hinge forward from your hips, dropping your torso down parallel to the ground. Reach both hands down to rest on your shin.

035 Intense Side Stretch Pose Arms Extended

The main focus of this stretch is the front-leg hamstrings. A side benefit of this pose is the stretch of the back-leg hamstrings, caused by the positions of the pelvis, hips, and back foot.

- Step your left foot about 3 feet (90 cm) ahead of your right foot, with heel-to-heel alignment.
- Exhaling, hinge forward from your hips, dropping your torso parallel to the ground. Reach both arms straight out ahead.

036 Revolved Intense Side Stretch Pose

Step your left foot about 3 feet (90 cm) ahead of your right foot, with heel-to-heel alignment. On an exhale, hinge forward from your hips, dropping your torso down parallel to the ground. Once balanced, twist your torso all the way to the left. Reach your right arm around your left thigh and press your palms together in front of your chest.

037 Bound Extended Triangle

Step your right foot ahead of your left foot. Exhaling, hinge forward from your hips, dropping your torso parallel to the floor. Reach your left arm behind your back and toward your opposite hip, and your right arm around your front thigh. Bind your hands.

Good Form
Keep your hips stable and squared up to the front of your yoga mat as you twist from your spine, not your hips.

038 Revolved Prayer Hands

Step your left foot about 3 feet (90 cm) ahead of your right foot. Exhaling, hinge forward from your hips, dropping your torso down parallel to the ground. Once balanced, twist your torso all the way to the left. Bend both arms and press your palms together in front of your chest in Prayer Position. Shift your gaze upward. When practicing poses in Prayer Position, make sure to keep your hands at the center of your chest, as they will tend to want to move toward one shoulder.

039 Revolved Bound Triangle Pose

Step your right foot about 3 feet (90 cm) ahead of your left foot, with heel-to-heel alignment. On an exhale, hinge forward from your hips, dropping your torso down parallel to the ground. Reach both hands down to rest on your shin. Once balanced, lift your hands from your shin. Reach your right arm behind your back and toward your opposite hip. Reach your left arm around your front thigh and bind your hands together behind your hips.

040

Half Moon Pose

Half Moon Pose is a standing yoga posture that will challenge your leg muscles and your ability to balance. This pose opens the chest, groin, and hamstrings while improving strength and balance.

tensor fasciae latae

obliquus internus*

transversus abdominis*

rectus abdominis

obliquus externus

serratus anterior

iliopsoas*

biceps femoris

semitendinosus

sartorius

vastus medialis

semimembranosus

Correct form
Attempt to lengthen your raised leg, pulling outward from your heel, and keeping your leg strong and engaged.

- Standing straight, step your left foot far forward and extend your arms straight out to your sides.
- Shifting your weight onto your left foot, begin to bend your torso forward and raise your right leg up from the ground. Continue until your back is parallel to the ground and your right leg is straight out behind you.
- Twist your torso to the right, placing your left palm flat on the ground and extending your right arm straight above you.

Avoid
Avoid this pose if you have low blood pressure or currently experience headaches, insomnia, or diarrhea. Those with neck stiffness should not turn their heads to face upward, but should instead continue looking straight ahead.

041

Half Moon in Prayer
Once balanced in Half Moon Pose (#040), lift your hand from the ground and bend both arms in front of your chest. Press both palms together firmly at the center of your chest.

042 Half Moon Reverse Prayer

Once balanced in Half Moon Pose (#040), lift your hand from the ground and bend both arms up behind your back. Press both palms together firmly behind your back in Reverse Prayer Position.

043 Bound Half Moon

Once balanced in Half Moon Pose (#040), lift your hand from the ground and reach it beneath your hips. Reach your opposite arm behind your back and bind both hands together behind your hips.

044 Half Moon Preparation

For an easier modification of the pose, rest your hand on a yoga block rather than directly on the ground. This can help if it is difficult for you to straighten your supporting leg. You can turn the block onto its long or short side.

045 Half Bound Lotus Pose

Raise your right foot and bend it up. With both hands, pull your right foot up to your left hip. Keeping your right foot in place with your left hand, reach your right hand behind and around your back and grab hold of your right foot. Then, release your left hand and begin to fold forward from the waist, dropping your head and shoulders down toward the ground. Reach your left hand down to the ground.

046 Half Bound Lotus Half Moon Pose

This movement is a standing balance that quietens the mind and gives you a sense of poise. Physically, this movement increases flexibility in the shoulders, hamstrings, hips, knees, and ankles.

· Raise your right foot from the ground and bend it up in front of you.
· Reach with both hands and pull your right foot to tuck against your left hip. Reach your left hand back around your back and grasp your right thigh.
· Begin to fold forward from the waist, dropping your head and shoulders down. Place your right hand on the ground.

047

Warrior I Pose

Warrior I Pose is the first of the three Warrior Poses. This pose establishes strength and stability in the ankles, thighs, and back, while deeply stretching the front of the body. The physical posture allows for a deep stretch of the chest and lungs, invigorating the body. It also encourages focus and calm.

Annotation Key
Bold text indicates strengthening muscles
Black text indicates stretching muscles
* indicates deep muscles

Correct form
Keep your feet firmly grounded and your shoulders directly above your hips. Attempt to pull along the length of your spine and arms from your fingertips.

Avoid
Avoid twisting the knee of your back leg outward or inward.

deltoideus

serratus anterior

obliquus internus*

obliquus externus

rectus abdominis

rectus femoris

latissimus dorsi

sartorius

gluteus maximus

biceps femoris

vastus medialis

adductor magnus

- Step your left foot 3 feet (90 cm) in front of your right foot.
- Turn the toes of your right foot outward so they face the top corner of your mat and keep heel-to-heel alignment.
- On an exhale, bend your left knee, lowering your hips down.
- Raise your arms straight up from your shoulders, so your torso and arms form a straight line perpendicular to the ground.
- Hold this pose for 1 to 5 breaths.

048

Bound Warrior
From Warrior I Pose(#047), twist your torso to the right. Reach your right arm behind your back and over to your left thigh, and your left arm under the thigh. Try to bind your hands.

049

Warrior I Backbend
From Warrior I Pose(#047), bend your head and shoulders back into a deep backbend. Keep your arms extended throughout.

Benefits
Increases stamina. Strengthens shoulders, arms, thighs, ankles, and calves. Stretches groin, stomach, chest, and shoulders.

050 Warrior I Open Chest

From Warrior I Pose (#047), clasp your fingers together behind your back, with your arms straight. Lean back into a deep backbend, keeping your hands clasped.

051 Bowing Reverse Prayer Warrior

From Warrior I Pose (#047), reach both arms behind your back and press your palms together behind your spine in Reverse Prayer Position. Bend forward, bringing your chest to your knee.

052 Bowing Deep Lunge

Known as the Humble Warrior, this pose is said to teach us how to surrender as we bow into the pose. Unlike other Warrior Poses, which make you face the world, this forward-bending pose draws your focus inward.

- From Warrior I Pose (#047), reach both arms behind your back and grab hold of the opposite elbow with either hand.
- Keeping your arms bound, bend forward, dropping your head down toward the ground.

053 Reverse Warrior

From Warrior I Pose (#047), drop your head and shoulders back into a deep backbend. As you bend backward, drop your right arm down along your rear leg. Keep your left arm raised.

054 Tiptoe Warrior

In this variation of Warrior I Pose (#047), raise your frontward foot up onto tiptoes. Maintain this position throughout the exercise.

055

Warrior II Pose

Warrior II Pose is one of three Warrior Poses most often practiced in yoga. It often comes earlier in a yoga sequence than Warrior I Pose. It helps to establish inner strength and stamina while mastering physical stability in the legs, ankles, hips, back, and shoulders. It is a pose that opens both the hips and chest, allowing for improved circulation and vital energy throughout the body.

rectus abdominis

obliquus externus

vastus intermedius*

rectus femoris

obliquus internus*

transversus abdominis*

tensor fasciae latae

vastus lateralis

vastus medialis   sartorius   biceps femoris   adductor magnus

Correct form
Keep your feet firmly grounded and your shoulders directly above your hips. Attempt to pull along the length of your spine and arms from your fingertips.

Avoid
Avoid leaning in front of your hips. Avoid arching your lower back.

· Step your left foot about 3 feet (90 cm) behind your right foot. Turn your left foot out to a 90-degree angle.
· Slowly bend your right knee, lowering your hips.
· Lift your torso so that your spine is long and your shoulders are directly above your hips.
· Extend both arms out to your sides, parallel to the floor.
· Find a neutral position and maintain this pose for 1 to 5 breaths.

056 Bound Revolved Son of Anjani
From Warrior II Pose (#055), drop your torso down and twist your spine to the right. Reach your right arm behind your back and hips. Reach your left arm between your hips and bind your hands.

057 Revolved Son of Anjani in Prayer
From Warrior II Pose (#055), drop your torso down and twist your spine to the right. Bend both arms in front of your chest and press your palms together. Hook your left elbow outside your right knee.

058 Fighting Warrior II

With all Warrior Poses you practice cultivating the mind of a warrior—staying unattached to the outcome as you strive to remain centered and work through your physical, mental, and emotional limitations.

- From Warrior II Pose (#055), bend your rear knee down toward the ground.
- Twist your torso all the way to the left and drop your right elbow down to your right knee.
- Keep your right arm extended and shift your gaze upward.

059 Hands on Hips

From Warrior II Pose (#055), rest both hands on the back of your hips. Gently press your hips into a more deeply opening stance.

060 Bowing Warrior II

From Warrior II Pose (#055), bend your torso and shoulders down toward your front knee into a bowing position.

061 Bowing Warrior II with Raised Bound Hands

From Warrior II Pose (#055), reach your arms behind you and clasp your fingers together. Attempt to raise your bound hands up along your spine. Keeping your hands clasped, drop your head and shoulders down toward the ground.

062

Warrior III Pose

Annotation Key
Bold text indicates strengthening muscles
Black text indicates stretching muscles
* indicates deep muscles

Correct form
Keep your hips squared and attempt to pull along the length of your body from your raised heel to your fingertips.

Avoid
Don't allow your lifted leg to bend or lose energy.

deltoideus posterior

trapezius

rhomboideus*

gluteus maximus

obliquus externus

obliquus internus*

rectus abdominis

transversus abdominis*

biceps femoris

gastrocnemius

Warrior III Pose is one of three main Warrior Poses. Warrior III is an intermediate balancing pose. This dynamic standing posture creates stability throughout your entire body by integrating all of the muscles throughout your core, arms, and legs. It strengthens the whole back side of the body, including the shoulders, hamstrings, calves, ankles, and back. It also strengthens the abdominal muscles. It improves balance, posture, and coordination.

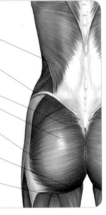

latissimus dorsi

gluteus medius*

piriformis*

gluteus maximus

quadratus femoris*

obturator internus*

obturator externus*

- Starting in Mountain Pose (#001), step your left foot forward. Raise both arms straight up from your shoulders.
- Lift your right heel upward, grounding your weight onto your left foot.
- Keep your right leg straight and supportive and square your hips before beginning to hinge your torso forward and raising your right leg straight behind you.
- Keep your arms extended over your head throughout.

Benefits
Improves balance. Strengthens ankles, calves, thighs, spine, core muscles, and shoulders. Stretches thighs.

Arms at Sides

During this variation of Warrior III Pose (#062), keep your arms down at your sides throughout the pose. This will provide a more challenging version of the balancing position.

Warrior Reverse Prayer

From Arms at Sides (#063), raise both arms behind your back and press your palms together in Reverse Prayer Position. Keeping your arms in this position, begin to fold forward into Warrior III Pose (#062), bending deeper still and raising your leg in line with your torso.

065 Wrapped Arms

From Warrior III Pose (#062), raise left leg above your head, toes straight out, and bend both elbows at right angles from your upper arms. Wrap your right forearm around your left forearm.

066 Half Lotus

During this variation of Warrior III Pose (#062), raise your left foot up to your hips and tuck the sole of your foot against your right thigh. Once balanced, extend your arms straight above your head and begin to fold into the Warrior III Pose.

- Learning to perfect the Warrior III Pose (#062) and its variations can be a challenging reward.
- Learning to balance in this pose requires strength and humility on many levels.
- Do not be afraid to fall! Simply try again. With patience and dedication, you will learn to face all of life's challenges with grace and determination.

067
One Leg Stretched Upward
From Warrior III Pose (#062), continue to bend forward, placing your hands flat on the ground in front of you. Bend further, dropping your head toward the ground and extending your leg further over your head. Keep your extended leg straight throughout.

068
Supported One Leg Straight Up
From Warrior III Pose (#062), continue bending forward and place both hands on the ground on either side of your supporting foot. Pull your forehead down toward your shin. Keep your extended leg straight throughout.

069
Unsupported One Leg Straight Up
From Warrior III Pose (#062), continue bending forward and place both hands on the back of your supporting ankle. Pull your forehead down toward your shin. Keep your extended leg straight throughout.

070
Bowing with Respect Pose 1

From Warrior III Pose (#062), bend your raised leg into your chest. Grab your toe with your hand on the same side and extend your bound arm and leg out to your side. Keep your opposite arm extended to the opposite side.

- In addition to balance and strength in the leg muscles, this pose can provide a deep hip-opening variation.
- Tight hips can manifest in lower back pain, muscle stiffness, and inability to walk the distances we once were able to walk with ease.
- For people who sit for long periods at work, the hip flexors and rotators become tight and the gluteal muscles weaken. This combination can quickly detract from our ability to walk, and to maintain good posture and the stability of the spine.
- Hip-openers can help remedy these muscle imbalancs, and increase the range of motion in the hips.

Namaste
Nama means "bow," *as* means "I," and *te* means "you." Therefore, Namaste means "I bow to you." To perform Namaste, you place the hands together at the center of the chest at heart level, close the eyes, and bow the head.
This is an act of deep respect.

071 Bowing with Respect Pose 2

From Warrior III Pose (#062), bend your raised leg into your chest. Grab your toe with your hand on the same side and extend your bound arm and leg out to your side. Reach your opposite arm down to grab hold of your supporting foot.

072 Bowing with Respect Bird of Paradise Pose Preparation

From Warrior III Pose (#062), bend your raised knee into your chest before extending your leg out to the side, rather than behind you. Extend your arm on the same side, weaving it under your raised knee and out alongside your leg. Keep your opposite arm extended throughout for balance.

073 Bowing with Respect Bird of Paradise

From Warrior III Pose (#062), bend your raised knee into your chest before extending your leg out to the side, rather than behind you. Extend your arm on the same side, reaching between your hips and behind you. Reach your opposite arm behind your back and bind your hands together behind your hips.

074

Extended Side Angle Pose

Extended Side Angle Pose relieves stiffness in the back and shoulders. It involves the use of many essential muscle groups, including the legs, ankles, groin, chest, lungs, shoulders, spine, and abdomen. This pose lengthens the muscles along one side of the body, while stretching the groin.

Correct form
Keep both heels on the ground throughout this pose. Keep a straight line from your outstretched leg to your raised arm.

biceps brachii

biceps femoris

serratus anterior

obliquus internus*

rectus abdominis

tensor fasciae latae

pectoralis major

triceps brachii

transversus abdominis*

sartorius

rectus femoris

semimembranosus

rectus femoris

gracilis*

semitendinosus

Avoid
Avoid Extended Side Angle Pose if you have low blood pressure or currently experience headaches, insomnia, or diarrhea. Those with neck stiffness should not turn their head to face upward but should look straight ahead.

Annotation Key
Bold text indicates strengthening muscles
Black text indicates stretching muscles
* indicates deep muscles

· Stand with your feet shoulder-width apart. Extend your right leg straight out to the side, and lower your body into a deep side squat.

· Lower your left hand to the ground in front of your left foot.

· Extend your right arm above and across your head, leaning your torso deeply to the side.

· Raise your gaze up to the ceiling and hold this position for 15 seconds before alternating sides.

075 Extended Side Pose Preparation
Step your left foot about 3 feet (90 cm) ahead of your right foot. Keep your toes pointed in the same direction. Raise your hands above your head and press your palms together. Bend from the hips, bringing your torso parallel to the ground.

076 Angle Variation 1

This variation of the Extended Side Pose Preparation works the quads, hamstrings, and abdominals. Remember to keep your spine parallel to the floor as you hold the pose for 15 to 30 seconds.

Yamas and Niyamas

The ancient practice of yoga ascribes to eight "limbs" that can help you achieve union with the Divine. The first two limbs are *yamas* and *niyamas*. The five *yamas* (translated as "restraints") are forms of ethical rules akin to the Ten Commandments. The *niyamas* are characteristics to regard and cultivate.

- From Extended Side Pose Preparation (#074), with feet apart but facing forward, bring both arms back from the shoulders and bend your elbows.
- Place the right hand under the left bicep and the left hand under the right bicep.
- Hold for 15 to 30 seconds, then switch to opposite arms.

077 Angle Variation 2

Step your right foot about 3 feet (90 cm) ahead of your left foot. Keep your toes pointed in the same direction. Bend your arms behind your back and extend your hands into Gyan Mudra. Bend from the hips, bringing your torso parallel to the ground.

078 Both Arms Variation

Stand with your feet shoulder-width apart. Extend your right leg straight out to the side, and lower your body into a deep side squat. Raise your arms above your head and press your hands together into Prayer Position. Extend your arms above and across your head, leaning your torso deeply to the side.

079 Tiptoe Variation

Stand with your feet shoulder-width apart. Extend your right leg straight out to the side, and lower your body into a deep side squat. Raise your left foot up onto tiptoes. Lower your left hand to the ground beside your foot and lean your torso deeply to the side.

080 Tiptoe Arms Extended Variation

Stand with your feet apart; bend your left leg on tiptoes and shift it to the left side, while extending your right leg, foot forward, sole planted. Raise your arms over your head, palms together, and tilt your upper body over your left thigh, creating a straight line from the grounded right leg through your torso to your head and your outstretched hands.

081 Bound Extended Variation

Stand with your feet shoulder-width apart. Extend your left leg straight out to the side, and lower your body into a deep side squat. Lower your right hand to the ground in front of your right foot. Lean your torso deeply to the side and reach your left arm behind your back toward your hips. Raise your right hand from the ground and reach it to bind with your opposite hand.

082 Revolved Side Angle Preparation

From Extended Side Angle Pose (#074), twist your torso toward your front knee. Reach your opposite arm under and around your knee. Then, press your opposite hand against the other so your hands are in Prayer Position and bound around your front thigh.

Take Your Time

Some people begin yoga in their youth, and others much later in life. It can take years to master the practice, or even a single pose! When we attempt to force the body into a position it isn't ready for, it makes injury likely. While it is important to have goals to work toward, it is also important to understand yoga as a journey that takes time.

083 Revolved Side Angle Pose

The Revolved Side Angle Pose involves a great deal of twisting and stretching. It strengthens the legs, stretches the shoulders and upper arms, opens the hips, and improves our feeling of balance.

- Stand with your feet shoulder-width apart.
- Extend your right leg straight out to the side, and lower your body into a deep side squat.
- Lower your right hand to the ground on the opposite side of your left foot.
- Twist your torso deeply to the left and extend your left arm above your head, leaning down to your knee.
- Hold this position for 15 seconds before alternating sides.

084 Bound Revolved Side Angle Pose

This pose strengthens and stretches the legs, knees, and ankles, and stretches the groin, spine, chest, lungs, and shoulders. It also stimulates abdominal organs, increases stamina, and improves balance.

- Stand with your feet shoulder-width apart. Extend your left leg straight out to the side, and lower your body into a deep side squat.
- Lower your left hand to the ground on the opposite side of your right foot. Twist your torso deeply to the right, leaning down to your knee.
- Reach your right arm behind and around your back. Lift your left hand from the ground and reach it beneath your knee to grab hold of your opposite hand in a bound position around your knee.
- Raise your gaze up to the ceiling and hold this position for 15 seconds before alternating sides.

085

Twisting Chair Pose

Chair Pose (#012) is a standing yoga pose that strengthens the thighs, buttocks, and hips. This variation, with a twist, provides a greater balance challenge while stretching the spine, shoulders, and chest. This pose stretches the muscles along the sides of the body and in the shoulders, while twisting the lower spine.

obliquus externus

deltoideus medialis

obliquus internus*

rectus abdominis*

sternocleidomastoideus

deltoideus anterior

transversus abdominis*

gluteus medius*

gluteus maximus

biceps femoris

semimembranosus

semitendinosus

rectus femoris

trapezius
deltoideus medialis
infraspinatus
teres minor
subscapularis
teres major
latissimus dorsi
quadratus lumborum

Correct form
Balance your weight on your heels rather than the balls of your feet, to maintain your balance.

Avoid
Do not overarch or stiffen your back. Attempt to keep a slight curve in your lower back.

Annotation Key
Bold text indicates strengthening muscles
Black text indicates stretching muscles
* indicates deep muscles

- With feet together, bend your legs and lower your hips level to your knees. Raise your arms up.
- Twist your torso to the right and hook your left elbow outside the right knee.
- Join your hands in a Prayer Position and gaze upward.
- Hold for 10 seconds before switching sides.

086 Fierce Pose 1

Practicing the Twisting Chair Pose is a great way to help detoxify your organs, warm your core, and increase strength in your spine and legs. It can add variety to your practice and enhance your balance and focus in all areas of daily life. Challenge your physical and mental flexibility with a twist!

Simplified Variations

If your spine and shoulders are not especially flexible, or if you have a larger stomach or chest, it can be difficult to place your fingertips on the floor to the outside of your opposite foot in a Twisted Chair Pose (#085). Instead, place a block to the outside of that foot and rest your bottom hand there. Alternatively, you can bring your fingertips to the outside of your same-side foot, or add a block next to the same-side foot.

- Stand with your feet at shoulder-width apart and your knees slightly bent.
- Extend your arms straight above you, pressing your palms together.
- Arch your lower back slightly and lower your hips down slightly.
- Shift your gaze upward and lengthen your spine.

087 Fierce Pose 2

Stand with your feet shoulder-width apart and your knees slightly bent. Extend your arms straight above you, with your fingers spread and your palms facing toward one another. Arch your lower back slightly, bending your knees and lowering your hips down. Shift your gaze upward and lengthen your spine.

088 Revolved Fierce Pose

From Fierce Pose 2 (#087), bend both arms in front of your chest and press your palms together in Prayer Position. Twist your torso all the way to one side, hooking your elbow on the outside of your opposite knee.

089 Hands Bound Revolved Fierce Pose

This pose challenges your balance, increases the flexibility of the spine, and stretches the shoulders and lower back.

- With your feet shoulder-width apart, crouch down toward the ground.
- Reach both arms out behind your back and lace your fingers together.
- Attempt to raise your bound hands further up your spine toward your shoulders.
- Lift your ribcage, turning your gaze toward the sky.

090 Intense Wrist Stretch Revolved Hand Bound

Stand with your feet shoulder-width apart and your knees slightly bent. Lower your left hand down to the ground, pointing toward your toes. Reach your right arm behind and around your back to your opposite hip. Arch your lower back slightly, and twist your torso all the way to the right. Shift your gaze upward and lengthen your spine.

091 Revolved Pose Dedicated to Yogi Shankara

Stand with your feet shoulder-width apart and your knees slightly bent. Lower your right hand down to the ground to the left of your left foot. Reach your left arm up above your head. Twist your torso all the way to the left, shift your gaze upward and lengthen your spine.

092 Revolved Fierce Pose (Hands Behind Head)

Stand with your feet shoulder-width apart and your knees slightly bent. Bend both arms and place your hands on the back of your head. Twist your torso all the way to the left and hook your right elbow on the outside of your left knee. Shift your gaze upward and lengthen your spine.

093 One Hand Bound Revolved Fierce Pose

This is a deep, standing twist that challenges your balance and strengthens your legs and core. It is also known by various English names, including "Single Hand Revolved Chair Pose."

- Stand with your feet shoulder-width apart and your knees slightly bent.
- Crouch down toward the ground. Reach your left arm behind and around your back to grab hold of your right thigh or upper arm.
- Twist your torso out to the left and raise your right hand to your chest.
- Shift your gaze upward and lengthen your spine.

094 Revolved Both Legs Bound Fierce Pose

With your feet shoulder-width apart, crouch down toward the ground. Weave your lower arm behind your legs as your upper arm wraps around your back. Clasp your hands behind your back in a bound position. Lift your ribcage, turning your gaze toward the sky. Hold this position for 15 seconds before releasing and switching sides.

CHAPTER TWO

Forward Bends

Forward bends, both sitting and standing, are a key component of yoga—creating space and length in the spine; stretching the hamstrings, the calves, and the hips; and strengthening the thighs and knees. They also promote lower body flexibility and help practitioners find the correct alignment needed to sustain these, and other, poses. They calm the brain, ease stress, and relieve mild depression; stimulate the liver and kidneys; and aid the digestive process. In addition, they can reduce the symptoms of menopause and relieve headaches and insomnia.

095

Intense Side Stretch

Also called Parsvottanasana, this intermediate pose stretches the shoulders, spine, and hamstrings. It strengthens the muscles of the legs and is good for stimulating digestion. Avoid this pose if you suffer from high blood pressure or have a spinal injury or back problems.

deltoideus

iliopsoas*

gluteus medius*

latissimus dorsi

gluteus maximus

biceps femoris

semitendinosus

sartorius

vastus medialis

rectus femoris

vastus lateralis

soleus

Annotation Key
Bold text indicates strengthening muscles
Black text indicates stretching muscles
* indicates deep muscles

If you can't do the pose in Reverse Prayer Hands, cross your arms behind your back instead, hooking each elbow with the opposite hand.

Correct form
Make sure your chest is tucked up against your thighs after you complete the bend and that your neck is in neutral position.

Avoid
Do not lift your back heel off floor; do not round your spine as you lower torso to leg; don't turn your hips out to either side.

- From Mountain Pose (#001), bring your arms behind your back and form Reverse Prayer Hands.
- Exhale and step your right leg forward 3 feet (90 cm). Turn your back foot out slightly, turn your torso left slightly, and tuck your tailbone in.
- Exhale and lean your torso forward with your back flat; keep your feet flat as you draw your torso down to the right thigh. Hold for 15 to 30 seconds; repeat with your left leg.

096 Intense Side Stretch Preparation

This variation of the Intense Side Stretch works the core as well as the shoulders, spine, and leg muscles.

- With your legs positioned for Intense Side Stretch (#095), bend your torso and reach your right arm straight out over right foot with fingers forming Gyan Mudra.
- The left arm is cocked, with the hand resting fingers down on your left flank.

097 Intense Side Stretch Hands to Foot

With your legs positioned for Intense Side Stretch (#095), arch forward, foot pointing up from the heel, and raising your toes. Reach down with straight arms and touch your toes with both hands. Make sure to keep your back level and head upright.

098 Intense Side Stretch Hands to Leg

With your left leg advanced, lean your torso over your left thigh. Reach back with both arms around your forward leg to grasp the calf of your right leg. Hold for 15 to 30 seconds; repeat with the right leg in front.

099 Intense Side Stretch Forehead to Shin

Extend the spread of the legs from Intense Side Stretch Hands to Leg pose (#098) and reach down to grasp your left ankle with both hands, lowering your torso and bringing your forehead to your left shin.

100 Side Stretch Hands Down

This pose, like many forward bends, requires limberness in both the back and the abdominal muscles. Make sure to perform a few flexibility warm-ups first.

- With legs positioned for Intense Side Stretch (#095), have your left leg advanced, and fold your torso down over your left thigh, with forehead to shin.
- Place your hands, in Gyan Mudra, on the floor. Straighten your back, raise your head slightly and reach back toward your right foot.
- Hold for 15 to 30 seconds; switch to the right foot in front.

101 Side Stretch Revolved Prayer

Increase the separation of your legs. Lean forward, bringing your shoulders perpendicular to the floor. Weave your right arm under the advanced left knee and connect with your left arm in Prayer Hands.

102 Side Stretch Prayer Behind Leg

With your left leg extended, angle your torso over the left knee, with your head slightly raised. Wrap both arms around your left knee and form Prayer Hands, fingers facing up.

Heel-to-Heel Alignment

This refers to poses in which the feet are separated in a wide-apart stance. If you drew a line from one foot to the other in this position, the heels would fall along the same line.

103 Uneven Legs Tiptoe Intense Pose

This variation of the Intense Side Stretch (#095) involves an extended cross body reach, a move that is intended to work your abdominals, side muscles, and shoulders.

- With your legs widely extended, right leg advanced, and left heel raised, bend your torso at the waist with your back parallel to the floor.
- Extend your right arm straight up and reach down with the left arm to touch the floor; your hands should be in Gyan Mudra.
- Hold for 15 to 30 seconds; repeat with the left leg in front.

104 Revolved Side Twisting

With your right leg extended, lower your torso and square your shoulders to the right knee. Grasp the right ankle with your left hand, and your right toes with the right hand.

105 Side Stretch Hands Bound and Raised

As you perform this pose, make sure to keep your back from rounding and your head from sticking up.

- With your right leg extended and your torso touching your right thigh, bring both arms behind your back.
- Bend the back knee slightly; interlace your fingers and bring your straight arms forward.
- Hold for 15 to 30 seconds; repeat with the left leg in front.

106

Half Standing Forward Bend

Correct form
If your hamstrings are tight, bend your knees as you fold your torso downward; then try to press your knees straight.

Avoid
Do not roll your spine into or out of this pose. Compress the back of your neck as you gaze forward.

Also called Ardha Uttanasana, this beginner pose stretches the spine, hamstrings, calves, and hips; strengthens the spine and thighs; and improves posture.

- From Standing Forward Bend (#107), with your torso folded over your thighs, inhale and raise your head and upper torso away from your legs.
- Flatten your spine and straighten your arms, placing your fingertips beside your toes.
- Hold for 10 to 30 seconds.

gluteus medius*

piriformis*

gluteus maximus

biceps femoris

gastrocnemius

soleus

Annotation Key
Bold text indicates strengthening muscles
Black text indicates stretching muscles
* indicates deep muscles

107 Standing Forward Bend

This is the preparatory pose for the Half Standing Forward Bend (#106). It stretches the spine, hips, hamstrings, and calves; and strengthens the spine and thighs.

- From Mountain Pose (#001), raise your arms to the ceiling.
- Exhale, bend forward and sweep your arms down, as you fold your torso against your thighs.
- Bring your hands to the floor, beside your feet, palms down. As you exhale, draw your sit bones to the ceiling. Hold for 30 to 60 seconds.

108 Intense Stretch Pose 1

From Standing Forward Bend (#107), grip your right toes with your right hand and draw your leg upward, with the knee straight and the heel down. Keep your left fingertips on the floor for balance.

109 Intense Stretch Pose 2

This bending pose also includes a side stretch and crossover grip. Make sure to keep your head down and neck relaxed throughout the pose.

- From Standing Forward Bend (#107), with your right hand on the floor, palm down, reach over with your left hand and grasp the outer edge of your right foot, drawing it off the floor but keeping the knee straight.
- Hold for 15 to 30 seconds, then switch legs.

110 Intense Stretch Pose 3

From Standing Forward Bend (#107), bring your upper torso as close as possible to your legs and then reach back behind the outside of your calves, with your arms straight and fingers spread.

Bend Easy

As you bend toward your thighs, remember to keep your back flat and to tuck your abdominals in toward your spine.

111 Hands Under Feet

From Standing Forward Bend (#107), with your back rounded slightly, lower your hands in front of your toes; slide your hands, palms up, under your toes. Hold for 15 to 30 seconds.

112 Arms Crossed

This variation of Standing Forward Bend engages the shoulder, neck, spine, and abdominal muscles. If you have trouble reaching so far down, bend your knees slightly.

Mind and Body

The word yoga means to "yoke" or "unite." The discipline aims to bring the mind and body deeply into sync with one another through physically and spiritually binding practices. This is accomplished by combining the three main yoga components: breathing, posture, and meditation.

- From Standing Forward Bend (#107), with your head down and your torso touching your thighs, raise your torso slightly, so that your elbows are touching your shins.
- Cross your forearms, forming an X above your ankles, and tuck each hand, palms down, around the outer edge of the opposite foot.
- Hold for 15 to 30 seconds.

113 Intense Stretch Pose 4

From Standing Forward Bend (#107), spread your legs further apart, angle your torso away from your thighs, and wrap your arms below your lowered head, grasping each elbow with the opposite hand. Hold for 15 to 30 seconds.

114 Legs Crossed

From Standing Forward Bend (#107), cross your legs at the knees, and shift your torso forward, placing forward-facing, outspread palms on the floor to take a portion of your weight. Hold for 15 to 30 seconds.

115 Sideways Intense Stretch

This side stretch with one crossover arm works the muscles of the shoulders, sides, abdomen, and lower back. Try to keep your knees from bending.

- From Standing Forward Bend (#107), spread your legs apart; shift your torso to the left, right side facing up.
- Reach down with your left arm; clasp the front of your right ankle with your left hand.
- Drape your right arm over the side of your head and reach down to the outer left ankle. Hold for 15 to 30 seconds.

116 Tiptoe Intense Pose 1

From Standing Forward Bend (#107), spread your legs apart and, as you rise up on tiptoes, reach back between your legs and touch the floor with your fingertips, palms facing forward. Hold for 15 to 30 seconds.

117 Tiptoe Intense Pose 2

From Standing Forward Bend (#107), place your hands on the floor, palms down, shoulder-width apart. At the same time, raise your torso up by standing on tiptoes, with your toes curled away from you. Hold for 15 to 30 seconds.

118

Wide Legged Forward Bend

Also known as Prasarita Padottanasana, this beginner pose enables you to stretch and strengthen your hamstrings, groin, and spine. If you have trouble reaching the floor at first, widen your stance or use blocks for support. Avoid the pose if you have lower back issues.

Correct form
Contract your leg muscles and make sure to ground your heels throughout the pose.

Avoid
Do not bend from the waist; do not let your neck compress—keep the weight on your palms and feet.

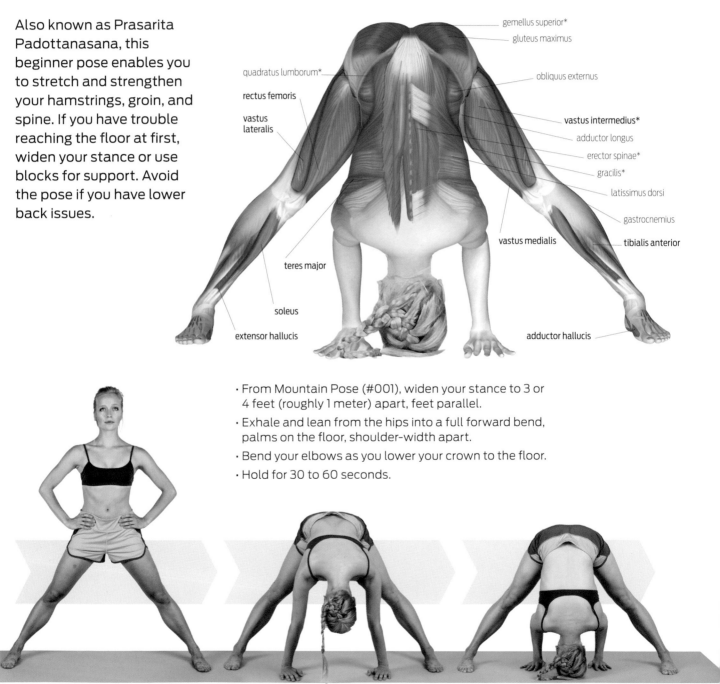

- gemellus superior*
- gluteus maximus
- quadratus lumborum*
- obliquus externus
- rectus femoris
- vastus lateralis
- vastus intermedius*
- adductor longus
- erector spinae*
- gracilis*
- latissimus dorsi
- gastrocnemius
- teres major
- vastus medialis
- tibialis anterior
- soleus
- extensor hallucis
- adductor hallucis

- From Mountain Pose (#001), widen your stance to 3 or 4 feet (roughly 1 meter) apart, feet parallel.
- Exhale and lean from the hips into a full forward bend, palms on the floor, shoulder-width apart.
- Bend your elbows as you lower your crown to the floor.
- Hold for 30 to 60 seconds.

119 Half Feet Out

In this variation of Wide Legged Forward Bend, make sure to keep your head down, crown facing the floor. Round your back, but keep your shoulders wide and open.

- From Wide Legged Forward Bend (#118), raise your torso up slightly by straightening your arms.
- Keep your head down, palms on the floor. Hold for 30 to 60 seconds.

120 Half Feet Out Backhand

From Wide Legged Forward Bend (#118), push your torso up slightly by straightening your arms. Keep your head down; place the backs of your hands on the floor, fingers forming Gyan Mudra and facing each other; angle your feet out to the sides.

121 Hands Behind

From Wide Legged Forward Bend (#118), shift your center of gravity onto your legs, while reaching back between your legs with both arms, palms flat on the floor, and fingers facing back. Hold for 15 to 30 seconds.

122 Hands to Ankles

From Wide Legged Forward Bend (#118), shift your center of gravity slightly back. Reach out with both arms to your ankles and grasp them from the outside. Hold the pose for 15 to 30 seconds, keeping your neck long.

123 Wide Legged Intense Stretch Reverse Prayer Hands

In this variation, you will rely on your legs alone to bear your weight. Shift your center of gravity back to your hips as you raise your arms.

- From Wide Legged Forward Bend (#118), elevate your head from the ground slightly and bring your arms behind your back, with elbows bent.
- Form Prayer Hands, palms pressed together, fingers toward your head, between your shoulder blades or as high up as you can reach.
- Hold for 15 to 30 seconds.

124 Wide Legged Intense Stretch Pose 1

From Wide Legged Forward Bend (#118), raise your head from the floor, shift your weight back, and place your hands, thumbs back and fingers forward, at your waist.

125 Wide Legged Intense Stretch Pose 2

From Wide Legged Intense Stretch Pose 1 (#124), release your waist and interlace your fingers behind your back. Reach out with both hands, away from your torso until your arms are parallel to the floor, if possible. Hold for 15 to 30 seconds.

126 Revolved Half Feet Spread Out Intense Stretch Pose 1

From Wide Legged Intense Stretch Pose 1 (#124), lower your straightened left arm to the floor, palm down and fingers facing left, and raise your right arm overhead, fingers pointing to the ceiling.

127 Revolved Half Feet Spread Out Intense Stretch Pose 2

This group of bending poses is also known as Parivritta Arda Prasarita Padottanasana. They are especially good for improving your sense of balance.

- From Wide Legged Intense Stretch Pose 1 (#124), shift your weight forward and lower your left elbow to the floor.
- Raise your right arm straight up from the shoulder, fingers pointing to the ceiling.
- Turn your head to gaze at your right hand.
- Hold the pose for 15 to 30 seconds; then use opposite arms.

128 Tiptoe Half Feet Spread Out Intense Stretch Pose

From Wide Legged Intense Stretch Pose 1 (#124), shift your weight forward as you place your straightened arms on the floor, palms down, and rise up on your tiptoes.

129

Seated Forward Bend

Also called Paschimottanasana, this beginner pose stretches the shoulders, spine, and hamstrings. It is known to stimulate digestion, relieve stress and headaches, and can even reduce high blood pressure. Avoid this pose with back injuries or diarrhea.

biceps femoris   semitendinosus

Correct form
To help you bend forward at first, try putting a folded blanket under your buttocks.

Avoid
Try not to round your back as you bend; don't force your torso downward.

To best achieve this pose, make sure you lengthen your spine from your neck down to your hips. Keep your neck in neutral position.

- From sitting in Staff Pose (#381), rock back and forth to draw the sit bones away from your heels.
- Inhale, and lift your arms straight up. Exhale, and stretch your sternum forward, bending from the hips.
- Lower your abdomen to your thighs, forehead to shins, and grasp your soles or ankles. Hold for 1 to 3 minutes.

130 Western Intense Stretch Pose

This variation of the Seated Forward Bend focuses on stretching the shoulders, ankles, and toes, while it releases the lower back.

- From Seated Forward Bend (#129), with your hands grasping your toes, sit up slightly with your head between your arms.
- Bend your elbows and extend your toes toward your upper torso.
- Lower your forehead to your shins and flex your toes forward, straightening your arms.
- Hold for 1 to 3 minutes.

131 Hands Over Heels

From Seated Forward Bend (#129), with your abdomen on your thighs, forehead on your shins, and elbows on the floor, tip your feet forward slightly and reach with both hands to grasp your heels. Hold for 1 to 3 minutes.

132 Hands to Ground

From Seated Forward Bend (#129), round your back and lower your chest to your legs, with your face to your upper shins. Place your forearms on the floor, palms facing down. Hold for 30 to 60 seconds.

133 Seated Forward Bend Prayer

From Seated Forward Bend (#129), raise your head and torso slightly, and reach back with both arms to form Prayer Hands, palms pressed together, at the center of your back. Hold for 15 to 30 seconds.

Stay Relaxed

When bending forward with your hands in Reverse Prayer position, it is not necessary to touch your face to your knees. Keep your neck relaxed and extended; don't let your chin sink to your chest.

134 Two Hands Revolved

This variation bending pose opens the chest and shoulders and allows your side muscles to stretch. Remember to keep your sit bones grounded as you twist.

- From Staff Pose (#381), circle your arms around your head.
- Lean into a left-side twist, touching your left toes with your right hand and your right sole with your left hand.

135 Seated Forward Bend Half Bound Lotus

From Staff Pose (#381), tuck your left foot atop your right thigh. Raise your right arm straight up, fingers in Gyan Mudra. Bring your left arm behind your back and stretch to reach for your left toes with your fingers.

136 Three Limbed Face to Foot Pose

From Seated Forward Bend (#129), bend your left knee and bring your left calf beside your thigh. Keep your forehead touching your right leg, as you stretch your arms forward and plant your palms on either side of your right foot.

Don't Sit on It
In this variation, you should not sit down on your bent leg; it should be positioned beside your thigh, knee angled slightly out.

137 Seated Head to Knee Pose

From Seated Forward Bend (#129), tuck your right leg against your left inner thigh, in Half Lotus pose (#066), keeping your forehead on your left knee or shin. Stretch your arms forward, hands in Gyan Mudra, to just beyond your left foot.

138 Churning Pose

In this twisting pose, make sure to keep your head position parallel to your advanced arm, and don't sink your chin to your chest.

- From Staff Pose (#381), bend your left leg and bring it beside your left thigh.
- Twist your torso to the right, bringing your left palm to the right outer heel, lowering your head along your arm, and bringing your right arm back from the shoulder, fingers pointing backward.
- Keep your sit bones grounded. Hold for 15 to 30 seconds; switch position.

139 Half Cow Face Western Intense Stretch Pose

From Staff Pose (#381), bring your left calf straight across your right thigh, foot pointed. Round your back, lower your head, and reach forward to grasp your right foot. Then place your palms on the floor beside your foot and hold for 15 to 30 seconds, before reversing legs.

140

Child's Pose

This beginner pose, also called Balasana, stretches the spine, hips, thighs, and ankles, and relieves stress.

- Kneel on the floor with your hips over your knees. Bring your feet together, fold your torso down onto your legs, and elongate your neck and spine.
- Place your hands, palms up, on the floor beside your feet.
- Allow your shoulders to widen and relax, and place your forehead on the floor.

Correct form
Inhale into the back of your ribcage; round your back so that it forms a dome shape.

Avoid
Do not compress the back of your neck; keep it extended, with your crown facing forward.

Annotation Key
Bold text indicates strengthening muscles
Black text indicates stretching muscles
* indicates deep muscles

latissimus dorsi

gluteus maximus

deltoideus posterior

teres major

serratus anterior

141

Child's Pose with Extended Arms
From Child's Pose (#140), with body folded and resting on your thighs, reach both arms forward, wider than shoulder width, and press the floor with your palms. Hold for 30 to 60 seconds.

142

Child's Pose Hands to the Side
While in Child's Pose with Extended Arms (#141), shift your torso to the right from the waist and reach your arms to the right, palms to the floor. Hold for 30 to 60 seconds, then reach your arms to the left side.

143 Child's Pose Palms Together

While in Child's Pose (#140), with your torso resting on your thighs, prop yourself up with your elbows placed below your shoulders and press your palms together in Prayer Position, with the outer edges of your hands resting on the floor.

144 Revolved Side Child's Pose

From basic Child's Pose (#140), raise your hips and buttocks, and twist your upper torso from the waist to rest on your left shoulder. Slide your left arm straight along your right leg palm up, and extend your right arm straight out along the floor, palm down.

145 Both Hands to Legs Bound Revolved Child's Pose

Twist to the right from Child's Pose (#140), shoulders now perpendicular to the floor and buttocks slightly raised. Reach out with your left hand to your right ankle and reach behind your back with your right hand for your left leg.

146 Reverse Child's Pose Dedicated to Garuda

This variation incorporates Prayer Hands—or Anjali Mudra—another of the symbolic Mudras, or hand gestures, performed during yoga.

- From Revolved Side Child's Pose (#144), wrap your right leg around your left leg.
- Press your palms together over your chest in Prayer Position.
- Hold for 30 seconds to 1 minute; reverse legs.

147 Child's Pose Sideways

Begin this variation in Revolved Side Child's Pose (#144), with your left shoulder resting on the floor. Hold for 30 to 60 seconds, then switch position so that your right shoulder and right cheek are on the floor.

Annotation Key
Bold text indicates strengthening muscles
Black text indicates stretching muscles
* indicates deep muscles

Extended Puppy Pose

The beginner pose called Uttana Shishosana, a cross between Child's Pose (#144) and Downward Facing Dog (#338), stretches the shoulders and spine.

- Kneel with your knees directly below your hips, hands shoulder-width apart. Bend forward onto your hands and knees, wrists below your shoulders.
- Exhale; press your hips back, lower your chest toward the floor, and extend your arms forward, palms flat.
- Relax your forehead on the floor while stretching your arms, spine, and sit bones forward.
- Hold for 30 seconds to 1 minute.

latissimus dorsi

rhomboideus*

gluteus maximus

biceps femoris

teres major

extensor digitorum

serratus anterior

Correct form
Slightly arch the upper back to provide your shoulders and spine with a gentle stretch. Also, elongate your spine in both directions.

Avoid
Do not rest your elbows on the floor, allow the middle torso to sink, or release from the pose too soon, or you may become dizzy.

149

Intense Extended Puppy Dog Pose 1
Shift your hips forward; place your bent elbows beside your head on the floor and bring both hands together at the back of your neck, fingers spread out.

150

Intense Extended Puppy Dog Pose 2
From Extended Puppy Pose (#148), shift your torso forward so that your hips are above your knees and extend your arms in front on the floor, palms down.

151 Water Grove Pose

In Extended Puppy Pose (#148), bend your legs toward the ceiling with toes pointed. Lower your torso onto your ribcage, keeping your hips elevated, and raise your chin. Rest on your elbows, forearms raised, with hands in Prayer Position or apart.

152 Water Grove Pose Hands Bound

While in Water Grove Pose (#151)—toes pointed up, hips elevated—bring your neck into neutral position, stretch your arms behind your back, and interlace your fingers.

153 Pose Dedicated to the Goddess Arani

Begin this variation pose in Extended Puppy Pose (#148), then arch your back, bend your knees, and point your toes straight up to the ceiling.

- Draw your arms up to your sides, elbows bent, and palms flat on the floor.
- Lower your chest and chin to the floor, and slide your arms along your thighs, palms up.

154 Lotus Intense Extended Puppy Dog Pose

In Full Lotus Pose (#415), tilt forward onto your knees, chin on the floor, and extend both arms, palms flat.

155 Eight Limbs Pose

From Water Grove Pose (#151), bring your lower legs down, with your feet on tiptoes. Then increase hip elevation, lower your chin to the floor, and bring your arms back beside your torso, elbows bent, and palms pressing down.

156 Feet Spread Wide in Inverted Locust Pose

From Eight Limbs Pose (#155), raise your hips up and spread your legs wide with knees straight; slide both arms straight back between your splayed feet, palms down.

157

Bound Angle Pose

The Baddha Konasana, or Bound Angle Pose, is also known as the Tailor Pose. This beginner pose stretches the inner thighs, groin, and knees. It can also help relieve the pain of menstrual cramps. It should not be performed with a groin or knee injury.

Correct form
Make sure to sit up tall, creating a straight line from sit bones to shoulders.

Avoid
Do not push your knees down with your hands or round your neck.

Annotation Key
Bold text indicates strengthening muscles
Black text indicates stretching muscles
* indicates deep muscles
biceps brachii
adductor longus
rectus abdominis
transversus abdominis*

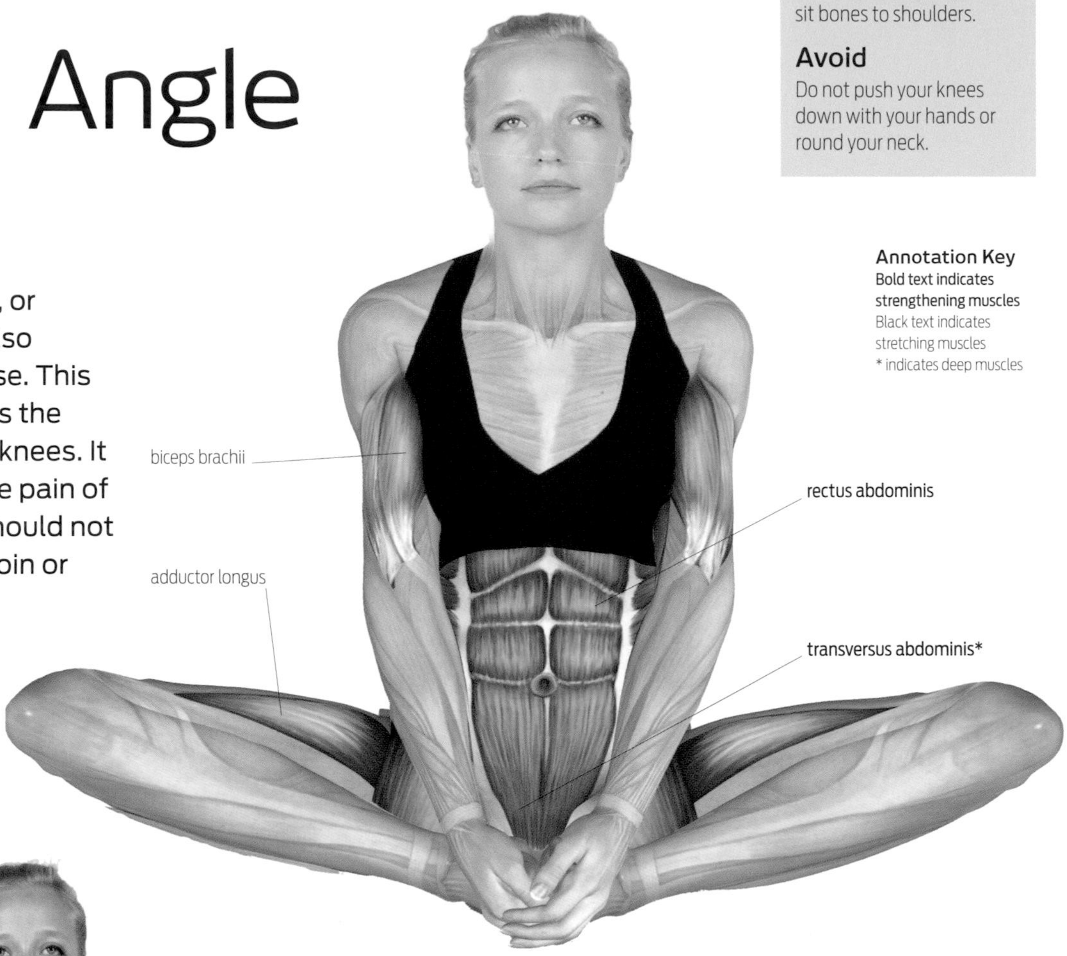

If there is thigh or groin pain, sit on a folded blanket to elevate the body. If you find the pose comfortable, extend it by bending forward, leading with your chest.

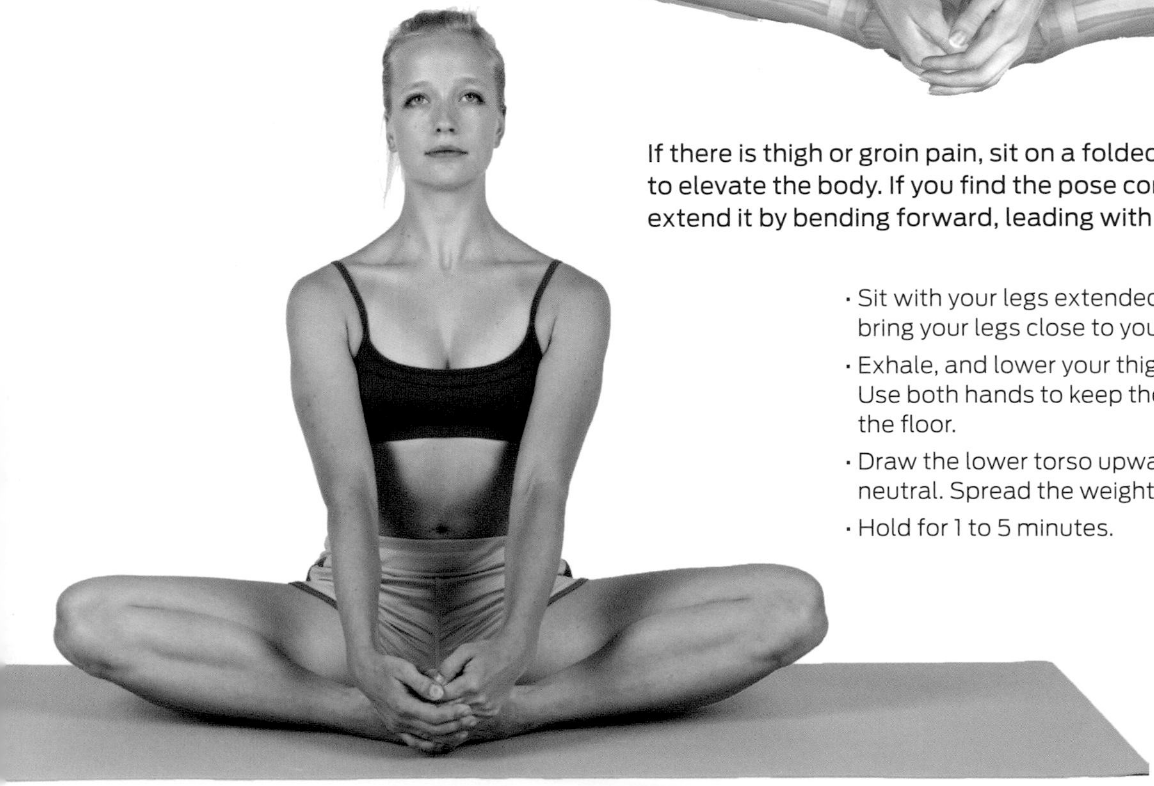

- Sit with your legs extended. Bend your knees and bring your legs close to your chest.
- Exhale, and lower your thighs outward to the floor. Use both hands to keep the outsides of your feet on the floor.
- Draw the lower torso upward, keeping your spine neutral. Spread the weight evenly over your sit bones.
- Hold for 1 to 5 minutes.

158 Bound Angle Pose with Hands in Prayer

While sitting in basic Bound Angle Pose (#157), draw your torso upward and, keeping your spine neutral, press the soles of your feet together. Raise your arms and press the palms together to form Prayer Hands at the center of the chest.

159 Bound Angle Pose, Bending Forward

From basic Bound Angle Pose (#157), with your torso elongated and spine in neutral position, lean forward so that your chest is over your feet. Hold for 30 to 60 seconds.

160 Bound Hands Bound Angle Pose

It is especially important to keep the spine upright and relaxed and to distribute your weight over your sit bones as you perform this extended pose.

- Sit with your legs extended. Bend your knees and bring your legs close to your chest.
- Exhale, and lower your thighs outward to the floor. Press the soles of your feet together.
- Place your left hand on your left knee and bring your right arm behind your back. Tuck your right hand, palm out, between your left arm and body.
- Hold for 1 to 5 minutes; reverse arm positions.

Muscle Focus

The Bound Angle Poses help to strengthen the back and make you aware of neutral spine position. Most of the variations work the iliopsis, the tensor fasciae latae, the adductor magnus, the adductor longus, and the ilacus muscles. If the inner thigh muscles, the adductors, remain tight, massage can help.

161 Bound Angle Pose Reverse Prayer

While in Bound Angle Pose (#157), press the soles of your feet together, and bring your hands behind your back. Press your palms together in midback, fingers pointing upward.

162 Bound Angle Pose with Cow Face Hand Position

This is another variation of the Bound Angle Pose that engages the back and shoulder muscles and increases flexibility. Be sure to keep your spine elongated.

- Sit with your legs extended. Bend your knees and bring your legs close to your chest.
- Exhale, and lower your thighs outward toward the floor. Press the soles of your feet together.
- Reach with your left arm over your shoulder and with your right arm behind your waist. As your hands meet, clasp your fingers together.
- Hold for 30 to 60 seconds; reverse arm positions.

163 Sideways Bound Angle Pose

Sit with the soles of your feet pressed together, left hand on left knee. Tilt your upper body and head to the right. Move your right arm back onto the floor, palm down.

164 Bound Angle Pose, Arms Extended Forward Bend

In basic Bound Angle Pose (#157), with the soles of your feet pressed together, reach forward with both arms and press your palms to the floor.

Don't Crunch
Remember to keep your neck long and in neutral position even when you lean forward.

Sit Bones

To get comfortable on your lower pelvic bones, lean them forward, inhale, then press the bones down into the floor as you rock upright.

165 Equilibrium Bound Angle 1

Balance is key in this pose, where your legs are off the floor and your entire body centers over your sit bones.

- Sit with legs extended. Bend your knees and bring your legs close to your chest.
- Exhale, and lower your thighs outward toward the floor. Press the soles of your feet together.
- Grasp your feet with both hands and raise your feet and legs off the floor, keeping your head, neck, and spine upright.
- Hold for 30 to 60 seconds.

166 Bound Angle Pose, Chin to Floor

From Bound Angle Pose (#157), while holding your feet with your hands, lean your upper torso forward over your feet until your chest and chin are on the floor.

167 Bound Angle Pose, Palms Together Overhead

In this variation of the Bound Angle Pose (#157), roll forward, rounding your spine, and tuck your head toward your abdomen. Fold your arms above your head in Prayer Position. Your legs should remain in the same position.

168

Fire Log Pose

Also called Agnistambhasana, the Fire Log Pose is an intermediate pose that stretches the groin and hip muscles. If you feel discomfort when bringing the bottom ankle under the top knee, tuck your lower foot back toward hip. This pose should not be attempted by anyone with a knee or groin injury.

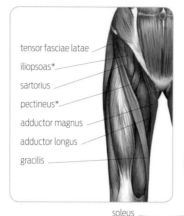

tensor fasciae latae
iliopsoas*
sartorius
pectineus*
adductor magnus
adductor longus
gracilis

soleus

Annotation Key
Bold text indicates strengthening muscles
Black text indicates stretching muscles
* indicates deep muscles

transversus abdominis*

quadratus lumborum*

Correct form
Make sure you rotate out from your hips rather than your knees.

Avoid
Do not allow your feet or ankles to rotate or "cave" inward.

- From Easy Pose (#388), place your right ankle on top of your left knee and your right foot on the outside of the left knee.
- Slide your left ankle below the right knee, so that your shins are stacked upon each other. Flex your toes.
- Raise your torso up on the sit bones, exhale, and let your hips open.
- Hold for 1 to 3 minutes; repeat with leg position reversed.

169 Accomplished One Pose
From Fire Log Pose (#168), with shins stacked and torso elevated, rest your hands on your knees and then bring them into Gyan Mudra, palms out. Hold for 1 to 3 minutes.

170 Fire Log Pose Fingertips to Ground

From Fire Log Pose (#168), spread your hands behind you, resting on the fingertips. Bend forward at the waist, keeping your fingers on the floor.

171 Revolved Fire Log Pose

This variation stretches the shoulder, chest, and side muscles.

- From Fire Log Pose (#168), form Prayer Hands at the center of your chest.
- Rotate your torso from the waist, first to the right, then to the left, dipping the left, then the right shoulder.
- Maintain Prayer Hands.

172 Revolved Bound Fire Log Pose 1

From Fire Log Pose (#168), place your right elbow on your left knee, with your hand forming Gyan Mudra; wrap your left arm behind your lower back, reaching for your right thigh. Repeat in the opposite direction.

173 Revolved Bound Fire Log Pose 2

From basic Fire Log Pose (#168), lean your torso forward and to the left, with your forearms on the floor, shoulder-width apart. Shift upright and then lean to the right with your forearms on floor.

174 Fire Log Pose, Palms Together Overhead

Bend your torso forward in Fire Log Pose (#168), curving your back until your forehead is on the floor. Rest on your elbows and place your forearms behind your neck; press your palms together.

175 Hand Position of Pose Dedicated to Garuda in Yoga Pose

From Full Lotus Pose (#415), raise your legs and shift your weight back onto your buttocks; then raise your forearms and twist them around each other.

Wide Angle Seated Bend

soleus · gluteus maximus · gluteus medius · vastus lateralis

vastus medialis · vastus intermedius* · erector spinae* · rectus femoris

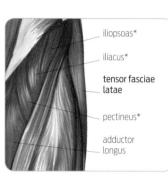

iliopsoas*
iliacus*
tensor fasciae latae
pectineus*
adductor longus

Also called Upavistha Konasana, the intermediate Wide Angle Seated Bend pose stretches both the groin muscles and hamstrings and also strengthens the back. It's important to keep your buttocks on the floor and not let them roll forward as you bend. Increasing flexibility in the waist and lower back will allow you to reach forward without moving off your sit bones.

Correct form
Make sure to keep your knees pointed up to the ceiling throughout the pose.

Avoid
Do not bend forward from the waist, but rather from the hips. Don't force your torso to the floor.

Annotation Key
Bold text indicates strengthening muscles
Black text indicates stretching muscles
* indicates deep muscles

- From Staff Pose (#381), separate your legs widely, turning your thighs slightly outward; flex your feet.
- Place your hands behind your buttocks, then inhale and push them forward to widen your legs even further. Press the backs of your thighs and sit bones to the floor.

- Place your hands on the floor in front of you. Exhale; bend forward from the hips, keeping your back flat. Walk your hands out and away from you as you lower your torso to the floor. Gaze forward.
- Stretch forward with your hands and torso without rounding your back.

177 Equal Angle Pose

From Wide Angle Seated Bend pose (#176), shift your torso forward from the hips, and rest your upper body on bent forearms, shoulder-width apart.

178 Big Toe Seated Angle Pose

From Wide Angle Seated Bend pose (#176), with your chest and your chin resting on the floor, extend both arms to the sides to grasp the toes of both feet.

179 Wide Angle Seated Arms Extended

From Wide Angle Seated Bend pose (#176), extend both arms in front of you and form Prayer Hands on the floor above your head.

180 Wide Angle Seated Reverse Prayer

From Wide Angle Seated Bend pose (#176), bring both arms behind your back and press palms together to form Prayer Hands, fingers facing upward.

181 Wide Angle Seated Hands Bound Raised

This pose stretches the shoulder and chest muscles and increases upper body flexibility.

- While in Wide Angle Seated Bend pose (#176), extend both your arms behind your back.
- Raise your arms toward the ceiling and clasp your hands together.

182 Equal Angle Pose Sideways

Follow the first two steps of Wide Angle Seated Bend (#176); raise your arms and cup the back of your head. Tilt your torso to the left and touch your elbow to the floor. Repeat in the other direction.

183 Both Hands to Foot Revolved

From Sideways Equal Angle Pose (#182), lower your hands from your head and reach out to grasp the right toes with both hands, keeping your arms rounded. Return upright and grasp the left toes.

184

Standing Split Pose

Also known as Urdhva Prasarita Eka Padasana, this advanced pose stretches the muscles of the groin, thighs, and calves, and strengthens the thighs, knees, and ankles. It is a valuable pose for improving balance. It is not advised for those with low back, ankle, or knee injuries.

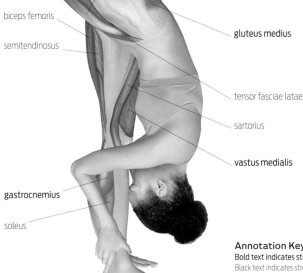

vastus lateralis

rectus femoris

vastus intermedius*

gluteus maximus

biceps femoris

semitendinosus

gluteus medius

tensor fasciae latae

sartorius

vastus medialis

gastrocnemius

soleus

Correct form
Make sure to lower your torso and lift your back leg simultaneously. Tuck in your chin and lengthen the back of your neck.

Avoid
Do not rotate your standing knee inward, round your spine, or bend forward from your waist.

Annotation Key
Bold text indicates strengthening muscles
Black text indicates stretching muscles
* indicates deep muscles

- From Mountain Pose (#001), shift the weight onto your left foot. Bend forward with your back flat; raise your right leg behind you.
- Exhale and contract the leg muscles as you fold your torso onto your left thigh; try to grasp the back of your right ankle with your left hand.
- Lift your right heel toward the ceiling; extend both legs in opposite directions.
- Hold for 30 seconds to 1 minute.

185

Standing Hands to Floor Pose
While in Standing Split Pose (#184), walk your hands out forward, palms down, until your back is nearly straight and your lower and upper legs form a line. Hold for 15 to 30 seconds, then switch legs.

Don't Rush
To avoid getting dizzy, always come upright slowly from any inverted poses.

186 Forehead to Shin

From Standing Split Pose (#184), reach your hands down to press both palms on the floor beside the supporting foot and press your forehead to the supporting shin. Hold for 15 to 30 seconds; repeat with other leg.

187 Standing Extended Variation

From Standing Split Pose (#184), increase the angle of the split by raising your leg toward the ceiling, with toes pointed; wrap both arms around the supporting leg. (To extend the split, try turning your hip slightly outward.)

188 Standing Unsupported

From Standing Split Pose (#184), point the toes of the raised leg, angle your torso away from the supporting leg, and bring your arms up behind you, extending them, fingers spread, so that they are now parallel to your back.

189 Standing Bound Unsupported

From Standing Unsupported pose (#188) on the right leg, raise your torso and twist to the right. Bring your right arm behind your back and your left arm around your thigh and behind your back; clasp hands.

190 Standing Half One Leg Stretch

From Standing Unsupported pose (#188) with arms stretched behind you, bring your arms forward and place your fingertips on the floor, shoulder-width apart. Extend both legs and keep your back and neck relaxed.

191 One Legged Downward Facing Dog

From Standing Half One Leg Stretch pose (#190), walk both arms forward until they align with your spine; the supporting leg is now angled forward. Lower your head between your outstretched arms.

CHAPTER THREE

Backbends

Backbends are an intrinsic part of yoga. They invigorate the body, uplift the spirit, and open the chest and heart. They can stimulate digestion and expose the body to deep diaphragmatic breathing. These positions can also benefit the health of the spine and vertebrae—keeping them supple and strong. Yet backbends also place demands on the most vulnerable portion of the spine, the lumbar region. Some instructors recommend "scooping" or "tucking" in the tailbone to prevent pinching, while others suggest engaging key core muscles.

192

Upward Facing Dog

This intermediate position, also known as Urdu Mukha Svanasana, is a prone backbend meant to lift and open the chest. Part of the traditional Sun Salutation sequence, it provides a lengthening and strengthening of the back, arms, and legs. It also aligns the spine and invigorates the kidneys and nervous system.

trapezius
infraspinatus*
rhomboideus*
teres minor
teres major
latissimus dorsi
multifidus spinae*
erector spinae*
quadratus lumborum*
gluteus maximus
gluteus medius*
adductor magnus

pectoralis major
serratus anterior
triceps brachii

semitendinosus
biceps femoris
transversus abdominis*
rectus abdominis

- Lie prone on the floor, with your palms flat, forearms perpendicular to the floor, and elbows close to the ribs.
- Press your palms on the floor, extend your arms, roll shoulders up and back, arch your back, push your chest forward, and raise the crown toward the ceiling.
- Inhale and lift your thighs and legs up from the floor, pressing the tops of your feet down.
- Hold for 15 to 30 seconds.
- Release the pose by exhaling as you lower yourself to the floor.

Correct form

As you rise, your shoulders, elbows, and wrists should be "stacked" in a comfortable line. In pose, imagine the lower tips of your shoulder blades supporting your collarbones. Firm the buttocks, but do not clench them.

Avoid

Do not round or raise shoulders, jut out your ribcage, dump weight on the wrists, or drop your thighs to floor. Do not perform if you have had recent back surgery or chronic injury to the back, hips, arms, or shoulders.

193 Upward Facing Dog Extended

Raise your upper body on extended arms, and with your hips, thighs, and legs on the floor, increase the arch of the back, extending your neck and easing your head into a backward tilt; your chin should be facing upward.

194 Raised Hips Extended

As you perform this variation, make sure to keep your neck relaxed. Don't crunch your head down into your shoulders.

- From Upward Facing Dog Extended Pose (#193), press your palms down, and tighten your back and buttocks.
- Raise your hips and legs from the floor.

195 Upward Facing Dog Reaching

While in the Upward Facing Dog Pose (#192), raise first the left arm and then the right arm above the head. This can be done with the knees on the floor or elevated off the floor.

196 Upward-Facing Dog with Uneven Legs

This pose increases the strengthening qualities of Upward Facing Dog pose (#192) throughout the lower back, buttocks, and thighs. Make sure not to let the bottom leg roll out to the side as you raise the opposite leg.

Sequence Options

Upward Facing Dog Poses can sequence from Table, Plank, Child, or Caterpillar Poses, and sequence into Downward Facing Dog, Child, Plank, Locust, or Half Bow Poses.

197 Upward Facing Dog Tiptoes

To raise your legs higher off the floor and increase the strengthening effect of this pose, curl your toes inward as you get into position.

Using Blocks
You can shift more weight to the lower half of your body by placing blocks under your palms before you attempt the pose.

- As you elevate your upper body by straightening your arms, curl your toes under your feet so that they are supporting your lower body.
- Press your palms on the floor, drop your shoulders, push your chest forward, and tilt your head back; raise your chin toward the ceiling.
- Breathe, and hold for 15 to 30 seconds.

198 Upward Facing Dog Sideways

Upward Facing Dog Sideways or twisting poses place extra emphasis on the abdominals, lower back, glutes, and side muscles and increase flexibility. Maintain the neck in neutral position and keep the shoulders squared. After holding the pose, return to Upward Facing Dog Pose, then reverse sides and rotate onto the other hip.

- From Upward Facing Dog Pose (#192), rotate the lower torso onto the right side, hips slightly elevated.
- Keep your legs together and straight, with toes pointed.

199 Upward Facing Dog Bent Knee

While in Upward Facing Dog Tiptoes pose (#197), press down with your forearms, firm the buttocks and abdominals, and bend the right leg, keeping your toes pointed upward. Raise the thigh as high as is comfortable. Return to main pose, then bend the opposite leg.

200 Upward Facing Dog One Legged Connected

This backbending pose, which evolves from the Upward Facing Dog Tiptoes, really engages the back, thigh, buttock, and shoulder muscles. Make sure to keep the thigh relaxed and the upper arm supple as you perform it.

- Assume Upward Facing Dog Tiptoes pose (#197) with head tilted back.
- Place your right knee on the floor, then bend it, and angle the right foot toward your right shoulder.
- Extend your right arm over your right shoulder, and reach back to grasp the toes of your right foot with your hand.
- Hold for 15 to 30 seconds. Repeat with the opposite foot.

201 Ankles Crossed Extended

While holding Upward Facing Dog Tiptoes pose (#197), cross one ankle over the other, so the lower body is resting on the curled toes of one foot. Press the palms down and elevate the legs and thighs. Hold for 15 to 30 seconds.

Stay Relaxed

Make sure to keep your neck supple and long in any poses that require the head to be tilted backward; don't hunch your shoulders up.

202

Cobra Pose

Also known as Bhujamgasana, the fundamental Cobra Pose can stimulate the digestive and reproductive systems, strengthen the lungs, and open the heart. The Cobra Pose also stretches the chest, abdomen, and shoulders, and strengthens the spine and buttocks.

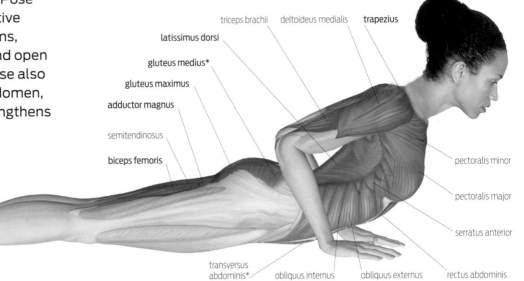

triceps brachii   deltoideus medialis   **trapezius**

latissimus dorsi

gluteus medius*

gluteus maximus

adductor magnus

semitendinosus

biceps femoris

pectoralis minor

pectoralis major

serratus anterior

transversus abdominis*   obliquus internus   obliquus externus   rectus abdominis

Correct form
Use your chest and back to create an arch in the back rather than depending on your arms. Do not completely straighten your elbows—that closes the chest.

Avoid
Do not tense buttocks or splay elbows away from torso. Keep your hips on or close to the floor.

- Lie prone with your flattened palms just below the shoulder, arms tucked close.
- Inhale and raise your upper torso, pushing down with both hands to guide you.
- Lift from top of the chest, push your shoulders down and back, and pull your tailbone toward the pubis.
- Elongate the neck and gaze slightly upward. Hold for 15 to 30 seconds.

203

Cobra Pose Hands to Knees
While in Cobra Pose (#202), reach back with both hands to the back of the knees, or grasp your kneecaps on the outside, while increasing the arch in your back. Tilt your head back and raise your chin.

204 Cobra Pose Unsupported

From Cobra Pose (#202), draw your right arm straight back from your shoulder, hand elevated, and palm up. Angle your head back, with chin up. Hold for 15 to 30 seconds; switch arms.

205 Cobra Pose One Leg Up

From Cobra Pose (#202), bend your right knee with the toe pointed forward, reach back with your right arm, and grasp the top of your right shin. Hold for 15 to 30 seconds.

206 Lotus Cobra Pose

While in Full Lotus Pose (#415), lean your upper body forward into Cobra Pose (#202), supporting your torso with both arms. Then reach back with your right arm and grasp your right ankle. Repeat with the left arm.

207 Cobra Pose Legs Bound 1

With your legs in Full Lotus Pose (#415) and upper body in Cobra Pose (#202), reach back with both arms and grasp both feet, while keeping your chest and shoulders up off the floor.

208 Cobra Pose Legs Bound 2

In this modified Cobra Pose, resting on your elbows with your back arched and your head upright, bend your knees, twist your left leg around your right leg and hold for 30 to 60 seconds. Switch legs.

209 Cobra Pose Legs Bound 3

In this modified Cobra Pose, start with the left leg twisted around the right leg, then switch to the right leg twisted around the left leg. The grasped foot should be the lower of the two—the one with the knee on the floor.

210

Half Frog Pose 1

Also known as Ardha Bhekasana, the Half Frog Pose opens up the shoulders, chest, and thighs. It benefits the thigh muscles and hip flexors, and increases the flexibility of the back. It stimulates energy, and prepares the body for backbends. This is a great stretch for runners and cyclists.

Correct form
Keep the knee in line with the hip. If there is knee pain, ease up on the pose. Tension should be in the interior of the thigh muscle, not at the knee joint.

Avoid
Don't slump into your shoulder or forward arm, and keep your neck muscles relaxed.

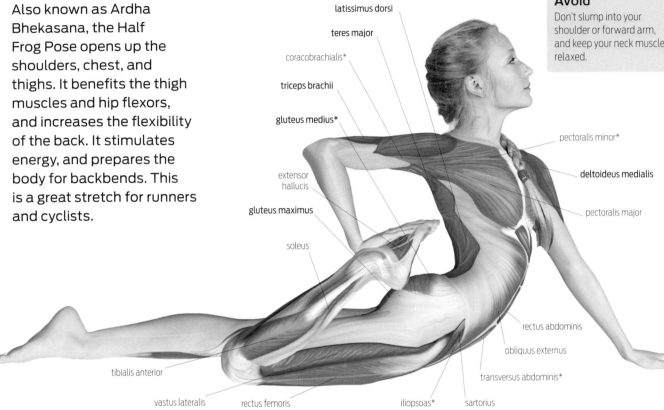

latissimus dorsi
teres major
coracobrachialis*
triceps brachii
gluteus medius*
extensor hallucis
gluteus maximus
soleus
tibialis anterior
vastus lateralis
rectus femoris
iliopsoas*
sartorius
transversus abdominis*
obliquus externus
rectus abdominis
pectoralis major
deltoideus medialis
pectoralis minor*

- Lie prone, with palms on the floor. Press your palms down and raise your upper torso from the floor.
- Soften the top of the right thigh; turn your fingers toward the front if possible, and also turn the right side of the body toward the front.
- Cross the left forearm in front of your body, bend your right knee, and reach back with your right hand, fingers forward, to the top of your foot, pressing it toward the outside of your right hip.
- Hold for 30 to 120 seconds, then repeat with the other foot.

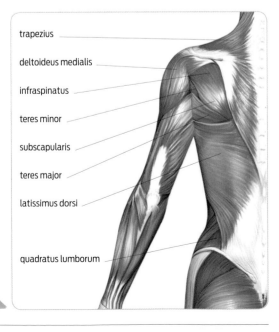

trapezius
deltoideus medialis
infraspinatus
teres minor
subscapularis
teres major
latissimus dorsi
quadratus lumborum

211   Half Frog Pose 2

This pose is similar to the Half Frog Pose (#210), but the hand position shifts from pressing on the foot to pressing on the ankle, bringing the upper leg closer to the buttocks.

212   Half Lotus One Hand One Leg

This pose requires flexibility in the back and shoulders and in the legs. Begin with the Half Frog to loosen up. Half Lotus Pose requires one foot to remain untucked and resting on the opposite thigh when in traditional Lotus Pose—sitting upright with knees bent and ankles crossed before you.

- Assume Half Lotus Pose (#416), the with the left leg untucked, resting on the right thigh.
- Lean forward on the untucked leg, so that the thigh of your right leg rests on the left foot.
- Bend your right knee and raise the lower portion of the leg.
- Reach back with your right arm and grasp the outer part of your right ankle. The forearm and lower leg should be aligned.
- Hold for 20 to 30 seconds, then switch legs.

213   One Hand One Legged Big Toe Pose 1

In Half Frog Pose (#210)—left leg extended back, right leg bent, toes facing up—reach back with your left arm and grasp your right big toe with your left hand.

214

One Hand One Legged Big Toe Pose 2

While in One Hand One Legged Big Toe Pose 1 (#213) increase the arch in your back, raise your lower torso and hips from the floor, extend your neck, and tilt your head back. Hold for 15 to 20 seconds, then switch legs.

215

One Hand One Legged Big Toe Pose 3

This variation of the Half Frog Pose really works the glutes, and the muscles of the back and shoulders. Remember to keep your neck in neutral position.

- While in Half Frog Pose (#210)—right hand on right foot—grasp your big toes and raise your lower leg into the air.
- Keep your back and upper thigh relaxed as you lift.
- Hold for 15 to 30 seconds, then switch legs.

Props and Aids
Beginners may support the chest with a bolster. If you can't quite reach your foot, try placing a strap around it.

216

One Hand One Legged Big Toe Pose 4

While in One Hand One Legged Big Toe Pose 3 (#215), grasp your right ankle with both hands and rock forward slightly onto your ribcage.

217 Half Frog Bow Pose

This intermediate pose enables you to open the chest, strengthen the back, shoulders, and abdominals, and increase flexibility in the legs.

- Perform the One Hand One Legged Big Toe Pose 1 (#213) with your left hand holding the right big toe.
- Shift forward onto your ribcage, bend your left leg and place your left foot on your right thigh near the knee.
- Reach backward with your right arm and grasp your left toes with your right hand.
- Hold for 15 to 30 seconds, then switch legs.

218 Half Lotus Frog Pose 1

While in Half Lotus One Hand One Leg pose (#212), with your right hand on the foot of your bent right leg, lean your torso forward into your left arm and press your right foot as close to your buttocks as is comfortable, with your right hand flat against the top of your foot.

Heed Pain

When pressing on a limb in any pose, always pay attention to pain, an indication you need to increase your flexibility. Never force a limb into a pose.

219 Half Lotus Frog Pose 2

From Half Lotus Frog Pose 1 (#218), grasp your right ankle with your right hand, lean forward onto your ribcage, reach back with left hand, and grasp the other side of your ankle. Your arms and leg should form a vee. Hold for 15 to 20 seconds, then switch to the opposite leg.

Bow Pose

The intermediate Bow Pose, or Dhanurasana, stretches the chest, abdominals, hip flexors, and quadriceps. It strengthens the spine and stimulates digestion. It should not be performed by anyone with a headache, high or low blood pressure, or back injuries.

Correct form
Spread your knees no wider than the width of your hips during the pose.

Avoid
Don't hold your breath—take short, controlled breaths. And don't roll back onto the pelvis to support your weight.

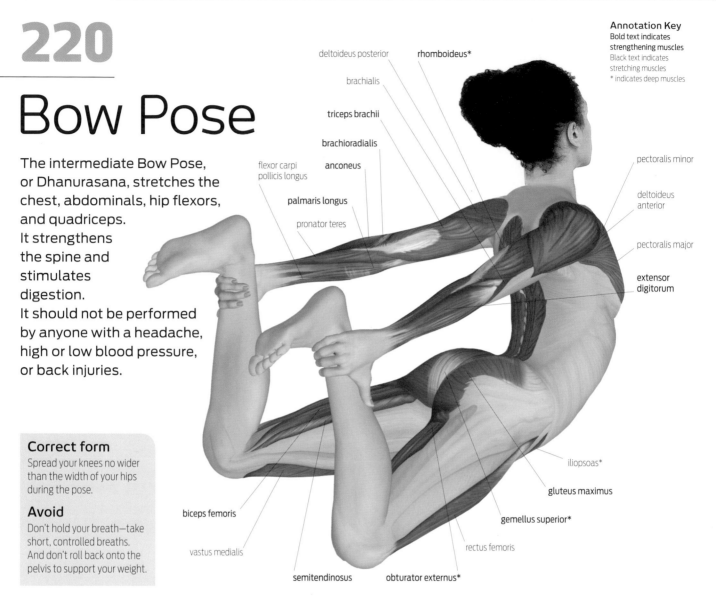

Annotation Key
Bold text indicates strengthening muscles
Black text indicates stretching muscles
* indicates deep muscles

deltoideus posterior
rhomboideus*
brachialis
triceps brachii
brachioradialis
flexor carpi pollicis longus
anconeus
palmaris longus
pronator teres
pectoralis minor
deltoideus anterior
pectoralis major
extensor digitorum
iliopsoas*
gluteus maximus
gemellus superior*
rectus femoris
biceps femoris
vastus medialis
semitendinosus
obturator externus*

- Lie prone with your arms beside your body.
- Place your chin on the floor, exhale and bend your knees, bringing your legs to your buttocks; reach back to grasp the outside of your ankles.
- Inhale, lift your chest off floor and raise your legs by pulling your ankles up. Shift your weight to the abdominals. Keep your head in a neutral position; keep the feet flexed.
- Hold for 20 to 30 seconds.

Grip Matters
As with many exercises, changing the direction of your grip can work a different set of muscles and tone different areas of the body.

221 Bow Pose Pointed Toes

Follow the instructions to achieve Bow Pose (#220), with your hands around your raised ankles, then point the toes of both feet upward.

222 Bow Pose with Underhand Grip

With any of the Bow Poses, if you find them difficult to begin with you could hold onto straps wrapped around your ankles, decreasing the length as you become more comfortable over time.

· Shift your grip from grasping the outside of the leg to an underhanded grasp of the inner ankles.

· Remember to keep your knees as together as possible, never wider than the width of your hips, and keep your weight over your abdominals.

223 Bow Pose One Legged Raised

In this version of the Bow Pose, hold your left leg by the toes and slide your right hand down your right leg and grasp the shin. Hold for 20 to 30 seconds, then switch legs.

224 Little Bow Pose

This version of the Bow Pose greatly opens up the chest. While in Bow Pose Pointed Toes (#221), slide both hands down along the shins. Arch your back and grasp the front of your legs as close to the knees as is comfortable. Hold for 20 to 30 seconds.

Stay Relaxed

When performing any backbend pose, remember to keep back, shoulder, and neck muscles from tensing. These poses need to be approached gradually, not during early sessions.

225 Sideways Bow Pose

While lying on one side, bend both legs back close to the buttocks, reach back with both hands to grasp your ankles, and pull your legs away from your torso while arching your back.

226 Bow Pose Toes to Elbows

In this version of the Bow Pose (#220), make sure to keep your neck relaxed; do not tilt your head back. The arching should take place only with your back.

- Perform standard Bow Pose (#220)—both legs raised and hands on ankles.
- Slide your hands along the tops of your shins, with the lower legs as close to the buttocks as is comfortable.
- Hold for 20 to 30 seconds.

Core Matters

While performing backbends, you should feel tension in your thighs, buttocks, and shoulders, but also in your core—the center of your body. This means you are engaging the muscles that support your torso and also aid balance and posture.

227 Bow Pose Big Toe 1

You will truly get extended here, so prep by doing several basic stretching poses. While in Bow Pose (#220)—legs raised, back arched, hands on ankles—slide your hands up to your grasp toes. Increase the arch of your back, extend your neck, and tilt your head back. Draw your legs high above your back, as far as is comfortable. Hold for 20 to 30 seconds.

228 Bow Pose Big Toe 2

While in Bow Pose Big Toe 1 (#227), bend your elbows forward and slowly draw your feet toward your head, making sure that the back, neck, and shoulders are relaxed. At end of the pose, your soles should be facing the top of your head.

229 Bow Pose Hand to Big Toe

While in Bow Pose Big Toe 1 (#227), release your left leg to extend behind you, toes pointed, and support your upper torso with your bent left arm. Hold for 15 to 30 seconds, then switch legs.

Extend
Continue to seek as much height as is comfortable with the leg and arm that remain in the air.

230 Bow Pose Hands to Foot Pose

Bow Pose has many variations. In this one-legged pose, you should feel tension in the inner thigh and buttocks, not in the knee. The hands can grip the big toe, all the toes, or clasp the top of the foot.

- In basic Bow Pose (#220), release your left leg to extend behind you.
- Grasp the big toe or top of your foot with both hands. Do not bring the raised leg down to your buttocks; try to keep it as upright as possible.
- Hold for 20 to 30 seconds, then switch to the opposite leg.

231

Bridge Pose

The Setu Bandha Sarvangasana is a versatile beginner pose that can be practiced in a variety of ways. It opens your shoulders and chest, strengthens the thighs and buttocks, and stretches the back, thorax, and neck. It can also stimulate digestion and ease stress.

Correct form
Be sure to roll your shoulders under once your torso is raised. Keep your knees positioned over the heels.

Avoid
Don't tuck your chin into your chest; don't use only the buttocks to lift—employ your legs.

Annotation Key
Bold text indicates strengthening muscles
Black text indicates stretching muscles
* indicates deep muscles

sartorius

rectus femoris

biceps femoris

vastus lateralis

transversus abdominis*

rectus abdominis

obliquus externus

deltoideus medialis

triceps brachii

gluteus medius

gluteus maximus

• Lie supine with your knees bent and your heels drawn toward your body.

• Press down through your feet and raise your buttocks from the floor.

• With your feet and thighs parallel, inhale and press your arms to the floor. Lift your hips to raise your torso from the floor.

• Hold for 30 to 60 seconds.

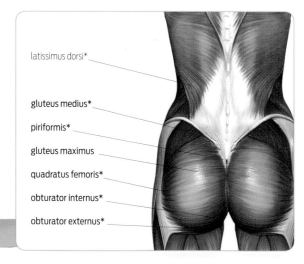

latissimus dorsi*

gluteus medius*

piriformis*

gluteus maximus

quadratus femoris*

obturator internus*

obturator externus*

232 Bridge Pose Preparation

Lie supine with your head in a natural position. Bend your legs and tuck them up against the buttocks; keep your arms alongside the torso and gently clasp an ankle with each hand.

Why Prep?
It often helps to do simple preliminary or preparatory poses before attempting a more complex, fundamental pose.

233 Bridge Hands to Back

This variation of Bridge Pose supports the lower back. Try not to splay your elbows.

- Perform basic Bridge Pose (#231), arms extended, palms down.
- Bend your elbows, raise your forearms, and place your hands just below your waist, cupping the top of your buttocks with the fingers facing up.
- Hold for 20 to 30 seconds.

234 Bridge Arms Overhead

From basic Bridge Pose (#231), with torso raised, arms parallel to the body, and back arched, extend both arms behind your shoulders so they rest on the floor, palms up and fingers pointing.

235 Bridge Hands Bound Below

From Bridge Pose (#231), with torso elevated and feet apart, bring your arms together beneath your body and clasp your hands together while increasing the arch in your back. Hold for 30 to 60 seconds.

236 Bridge Hands to Ankles

While in Bridge Pose (#231), with your arms on the floor, increase the arch of your back and reach your hands forward to grasp your ankles, holding the pose for 20 to 30 seconds.

237 Tiptoe Bridge Pose

In this version of the Bridge Pose, there will be additional pressure on your shoulders and neck. Remember to keep those muscles relaxed, and to extend your neck as much as possible rather than crunching your chin against your chest.

- While in Bridge Pose (#231), increase the angle of your torso and press down with your arms and hands.
- Raise yourself up onto pointed toes.
- Hold for 15 to 30 seconds or as long as comfortable.

238 One Legged Bridge Pose 1

Using the platform of basic Bridge Pose, there are several variations that allow you to work the large muscles of the lower torso and upper legs as well as strengthen the back and hips. In this version of Bridge Pose, make sure you are pressing down with both arms and the foot that remains on the floor in order to maintain the elevation of your torso.

- Start out in basic Bridge Pose (#231), then raise your right leg with knee bent and foot flexed so that your thigh is perpendicular to the floor.
- Extend your right leg at an angle so the right thigh is parallel to the left thigh, toes pointing.
- Hold for 20 to 30 seconds; repeat with the opposite leg.

239 One Legged Bridge Pose 2

While in Bridge Pose (#231), bend your arms up and cradle your hips in your hands. Once you are supported, raise the right leg straight up, with toes pointed. Repeat with the other leg.

240 One Legged Bridge Pose 3

While in One Legged Bridge Pose 2 (#239), brace your torso on your supporting leg, and move your hands forward to touch or grasp your ankles.

Prevent Wobbling

Your support in this pose should come from your shoulders, arms, left leg, and abdominals. Try to maintain balance and not wobble.

241 Tiptoe One Legged Bridge Pose

While in Tiptoe Bridge Pose (#237), extend the right leg straight up, toes pointed. If more comfortable, rest on your tiptoes instead of on pointed toes. Repeat with the other leg.

Upward Facing Bow Pose

The Urdhva Dhanurasana, also called the Wheel Pose, is an intermediate back-bending pose that strengthens the thighs and buttocks. It opens the chest and spine, stimulates digestion and thyroid function, and reduces stress. As you rise, make sure not to put all the extension on your lower back.

rhomboideus*
quadratus lumborum
piriformis*
quadratus femoris*
obturator internus*
obturator externus*
adductor magnus
semitendinosus
biceps femoris

transversus abdominis*
obliquus externus
rectus abdominis
gluteus medius*
gluteus maximus
semitendinosus
biceps femoris
vastus lateralis
latissimus dorsi
serratus anterior
teres major
teres minor
coracobrachialis*
infraspinatus*
trapezius
deltoideus medialis
biceps brachii
palmaris longus
flexor carpi radialis

Annotation Key
Bold text indicates
strengthening muscles
Black text indicates
stretching muscles
* indicates deep muscles

- Lie supine, with knees bent and heels drawn close. Place your palms on the floor beside your head, fingers facing backward.
- Press down with hands and feet to raise yourself onto your crown.
- Arch your back and extend upward; straighten your arms and legs as much as possible. Hold for 15 to 30 seconds.

Correct form
Extend through the shoulders, spine, and quads. Keep knees close together.

Avoid
Do not turn your toes out or splay your elbows to the side as you push up.

243 Half Bow Pose

Perform steps one and two of Upward Facing Bow Pose (#242), with your head resting on your crown and your buttocks on the floor.

- Move your hands to your navel and press them together with knees bent, legs raised on pointed toes.
- In that pose, raise your right leg parallel to the floor.
- Hold for 15 to 30 seconds; repeat with the other leg.

244 Upward Bow Pose Head to Ground

While in Upward Facing Bow Pose (#242), bend your elbows outward and slowly lower your upper torso so that your head ends up resting on the crown. The weight should remain on your feet and hands.

245 One Handed Upward Facing Bow Pose

This pose strengthens the thighs, glutes, and spine, while increasing energy.

- While in Upward Bow Pose Head to Ground (#244), elevate your legs onto tiptoes and then raise your right arm and reach straight forward to the right hip or thigh.
- Hold for 15 to 30 seconds; repeat with the other arm.
- Engage your core, and remember to keep your neck muscles relaxed. The upper weight should mainly be on the arm and hand.

246 Upward Bow Inverted Tiptoe

While in Upward Bow Pose Head to Ground (#244), rise on your tiptoes, increase the arch of your back, and reach backward with both hands to grasp or touch your ankles.

Camel Pose

The Ustrasana is an intermediate pose that opens the entire front portion of the body. It stretches the thighs, hip flexors, chest, ankles, and abdominals, and strengthens the spine. It can also stimulate digestion and the nervous system, and increase blood flow to the face.

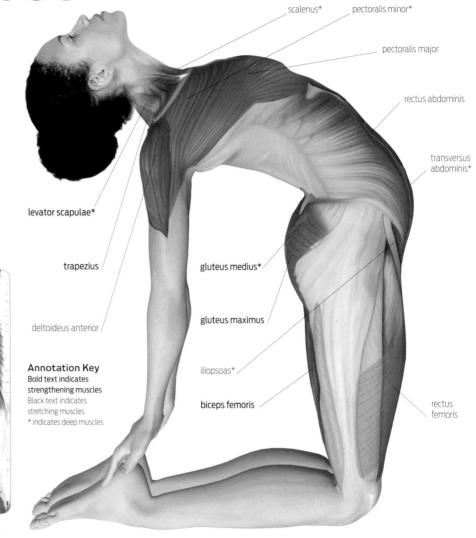

scalenus* pectoralis minor*

pectoralis major

rectus abdominis

transversus abdominis*

levator scapulae*

trapezius

gluteus medius*

gluteus maximus

deltoideus anterior

iliopsoas*

biceps femoris

rectus femoris

Annotation Key
Bold text indicates
strengthening muscles
Black text indicates
stretching muscles
* indicates deep muscles

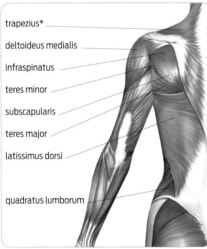

trapezius*

deltoideus medialis

infraspinatus

teres minor

subscapularis

teres major

latissimus dorsi

quadratus lumborum

- Kneel with your knees hip-width apart, tailbone tucked in.
- Place your hands on your lower back, fingers pointing down. Tilt your upper torso backward.
- Exhale and drop back, pressing your pelvis upward and elongating your spine. Press your shoulder blades back, lean slightly to the right, and drop your right hand to your right heel. Lean slightly left and place your left hand on your left heel.
- Center your weight between your knees, lift your chest as you arch, drop your head back, and relax your throat.
- Hold for 20 to 60 seconds. To release, contract the stomach muscles, lift the chest forward, and raise your hands to the lower back.

254 Camel Pose Preparation

Kneel with your knees hip-width apart, tailbone tucked in. Place your hands on your lower back, fingers pointing down. Lean your upper torso backward and gently drop your head back.

255 Prayer Camel Pose

From Camel Pose (#253), bring your arms slowly round and in front, keeping your back arched. Join your hands together in Prayer Position in front of your chest.

256 Camel Raised Bound Hands

This is an effective stretching pose that engages the core and works the muscles of the upper body.

Stay Balanced

Don't lean too far back or too far forward in this pose. There should be an imaginary line running from the back of your shoulder to the front of your hips. Arms should be elevated on either side of the chin.

- From basic Camel Pose (#253), ease your torso down and bring your buttocks closer to your feet, but do not rest them on your heels.
- Arch the back and tilt your head back on a supple, relaxed neck.
- Interlace your fingers of both hands and raise both arms high overhead, palms facing up, extending them until your elbows are straight.
- Hold for 30 to 60 seconds.

257 Unsupported Upward Salute Pose

While in Camel Pose (#253), with your back arched and your head tilted back, reach back with both arms, either palms apart or together, until the elbows are straight.

258 Knees Crossed Camel Pose

You should feel this variation of the Camel Pose in both your abdominals and your hamstrings. Try not to put too much weight on your arms—your core and legs should be bearing the brunt of the weight. While in Camel Pose (#253), your back arched, head tilted, and your hands reaching down to ankles, cross your legs at the knees. Adjust to the wider spread of your feet as you reach back to touch your heels. Hold for 20 to 30 seconds, then switch legs.

259 Extended Hand to Big Toe in Camel Pose

This variation of Camel Pose requires good balance and excellent flexibility. Make sure you have warmed up with some basic arm and leg stretching poses before attempting this pose.

- From Camel Pose (#253), swing your right leg out in front of you.
- Grab your big toe with two fingers and thumb and begin to raise your leg with your knee locked.
- Balancing on your left hand, swing your leg around and up as straight and high as you can comfortably manage.
- Hold for 10 seconds and repeat on the other side.

Improve Slowly

Never use brute force to achieve a pose; that's the best way to risk injury. Instead, work toward increasing flexibility and relaxing tense limbs.

260 Camel Extended Hands to Floor

While holding basic Camel Pose (#253)— your back arched and head tilted back—widen the position of your knees, and then reach back to touch the floor beyond your splayed feet with the fingertips of both hands shoulder-width apart.

261 Half Camel Pose

Use this backbend to create space in your front body and increase your energy and vibrancy.

- While in basic Camel Pose (#253), with your legs hip-width apart, place your left palm on the floor just beyond your left foot, fingers facing back.
- Then reach straight back with your right arm, thumb and forefinger forming a circle, arm parallel to the floor.
- Hold for 15 to 30 seconds; repeat with the opposite arm.

Mudras
The most common of the mudras, hand gestures, used in yoga is the thumb and forefinger circle. Called Gyan Mudra, it symbolizes fire and air.

262 Bed Pose

From Camel Pose (#253), lower the torso and rest your buttocks between bent legs; tilt your head back to rest on the crown. Support the upper torso on bent elbows, while your hands clasp your heels.

263 Bed Pose Arms Crossed

While in Bed Pose (#262), reach your arms back along the sides of the head and cross your forearms behind the top of the head. Shoulders and upper back should remain elevated and arched.

264

Fish Pose

The pose known as Matsyasana is said to enable one to float like a fish if performed in water. On land, it improves posture and strengthens the upper back and neck. It also stretches the throat, navel, abdominals, and the intercostal muscles between the ribs.

Annotation Key
Bold text indicates strengthening muscles
Black text indicates stretching muscles
* indicates deep muscles

Correct form
Keep forearms and elbows close to body; keep legs straight, bent, or in Full Lotus Pose (#415).

Avoid
Do not push weight onto the head or neck; do not lift hips as you push up into the arch.

obliquus internus*

obliquus externus

rectus abdominis

transversus abdominis*

serratus anterior

pectoralis major

deltoideus posterior

pectoralis minor

scalenus*

erector spinae*

latissimus dorsi

brachioradialis

biceps brachii

triceps brachii

deltoideus anterior

· Lie supine; slide your hands, palm down, under your buttocks.
· Press down with your forearms, bending the elbows and lifting your chest to arch your back.
· Tilt your head so the top rests on the floor; keep your weight on the elbows.
· Hold for 15 to 30 seconds.

Half Fish Pose 1

In Fish Pose (#264), bring your arms over your head and position your hands palms down, facing your torso. Bend your knees and press down with your toes.

Half Fish Pose 2

In Fish Pose (#264), bring your arms along the sides, palms down, and draw your heels in tight against the buttocks. Hold for 30 to 60 seconds.

267 Fish Pose Reverse Prayer

In Fish Pose (#264), with legs extended, bring your hands together under an arched back and press your palms together in Prayer Position, fingers pointing toward your head.

268 Fish Intense Leg Stretch

In basic Fish Pose (#264), with your head back, your back arched, and your legs extended, raise both arms forward from the shoulders and clasp your palms together in Prayer Position. Hold for 30 to 60 seconds.

269 Half Bound Lotus Fish Pose

In Fish Pose (#264), bring your left foot up to your right thigh in Half Lotus Pose (#416); reach under your back with your left hand and grasp your left foot. Hold 30 seconds; switch legs.

270 Fish Pose in Lotus

While in Fish Pose (#264), arrange both legs in Full Lotus Pose (#415). Rest your hands on top of your thighs and form the Gyan Mudra with both hands. Keep the back arched and head tilted back.

271 Fish Intense Leg Pose

Also known as Uttana Padasana, this pose is considered to be useful for stomach-related ailments. It is also thought to increase relaxation and to open the root and solar plexus chakras, which are associated with energy and willpower.

- While in Fish Pose (#264), extend your arms from your shoulders and your legs from your hips, keeping your elbows and knees straight.

- Your arms and legs should both be perpendicular to the torso, not angled straight up to the ceiling, and the head should remain tilted back.

Weight Watch
During this pose, make sure the weight of your raised and extended legs does not tip your head up from the floor.

Locust Pose 1

Also called Salabhasana, the beginner Locust Pose strengthens the spine, buttocks, arms, and legs, and is great for stretching the hip flexors, chest, and abdominal muscles. Like many backbends, it stimulates digestion. This is an effective preparation pose for performing deeper backbend poses.

Annotation Key
Bold text indicates strengthening muscles
Black text indicates stretching muscles
* indicates deep muscles

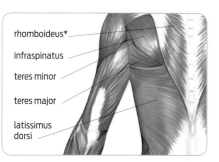

rhomboideus*
infraspinatus
teres minor
teres major
latissimus dorsi

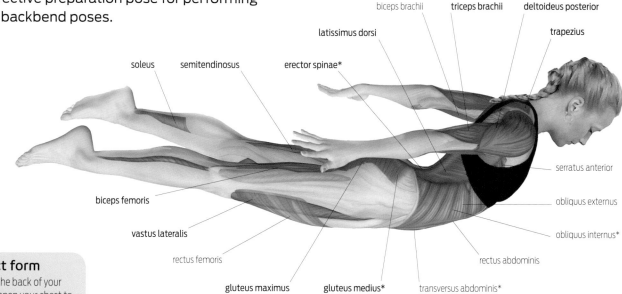

soleus
semitendinosus
erector spinae*
latissimus dorsi
biceps brachii
triceps brachii
deltoideus posterior
trapezius
serratus anterior
obliquus externus
obliquus internus*
rectus abdominis
transversus abdominis*
gluteus medius*
gluteus maximus
rectus femoris
vastus lateralis
biceps femoris

Correct form
Elongate the back of your neck and open your chest to extend the arch throughout the entire spine.

Avoid
Do not bend your knees, if possible, and avoid holding your breath.

- Lie prone on the floor with your arms at your sides, palms down. Turn the legs inward so that your knees point down to the floor.
- Squeeze your buttocks, inhale, then lift your head, arms, and legs at the same time.
- Lift up as high as possible, using your pelvis and lower abdominals to stabilize you. Keep your neck in neutral position.
- Hold for 30 to 60 seconds; repeat 1 or 2 times.

273 Locust Pose 2

This variation of the Locust Pose places emphasis on the lower body, especially the abdominals, glutes, quads, and hamstrings.

- Lie prone with your arms resting at your sides.
- Bend your elbows and position your hands, palms down, just below the shoulders.
- Inhale and simultaneously raise your head, chest, and both legs. Keep your legs straight, with toes pointed. Hold for 15 to 30 seconds.

274 Locust Reverse Prayer

While in Locust Pose 1 (#272), with your arms and legs raised, bring both hands to the small of the back and press your palms together in Prayer Position. Fingers should be pointing up toward the head, and the hands should be pressed to the spine.

275 Locust Pose 3

While in basic Locust Pose 1 (#272), with arms and legs elevated, increase the lift of the chest by reaching straight back with the arms, palms open, and tilting the head back into an upright position.

276 Locust Hands Bound

While in position for Locust Pose 3 (#275), shift your arms up slightly and extend; clasp your hands together at or near the height of the shoulders, trying to keep your elbows straight.

Good Tension
You should feel tension between your shoulder blades as you clasp your hands together; your chest will also open in this pose.

277 Superman Pose

Imitate the "Man of Steel" as he flies through the air—begin in Locust Pose 1 (#272), then elevate your head and move your arms to the front of your shoulders, and extend them forward, fingers spread. Try to maintain the previous elevation with your legs.

278 Inverted Locust Pose

Also known as the Grasshopper Pose, this asana strengthens legs and the upper and lower back. It helps to improve posture and can be beneficial in relieving stress. It is considered therapeutic for constipation and indigestion.

· In this variation, begin in Locust Pose 1 (#272) with your arms at your side, palms down.

· Drop your chin and chest to the floor while increasing the angle of your raised legs.

· Use your shoulders, arms, and torso to counterbalance your elevated lower limbs.

279 One Legged Frog in Locust

Lie prone, your chest propped up on your forearms, your legs extended behind. Curl your left foot to touch your buttocks, reach your left arm back and grasp your toes. Reach out with your right arm and form Gyan Mudra. Repeat with the opposite leg.

280 Pose Dedicated to Makara

While in Superman Pose (#277), with your arms raised and your legs fully extended, bend your elbows, bring your arms behind your head, and then interlace your fingers behind your neck. Do not let the pressure of your hands push the head forward; keep the neck position neutral. Maintain elevation in the legs.

281 Mermaid in Locust Pose

While in Superman Pose (#277), with your head upright, reach back with your left arm while bending your left leg toward your buttocks and grasp your left ankle. You can also raise both bent arms to shoulder height.

282 One Legged Inverted Locust

Start in a kneeling position. Bring your palms onto the floor with your fingers faced sideways on either side of your knees. Bend your arms and lean forward, putting the weight of your chest onto the backs of your upper arms, creating a tripod. Extend your left leg straight behind you, balancing on the top of the foot. Kick the right leg up into a split above you.

283 Raised Inverted Locust Pose

The Raised Inverted Locust is a very challenging pose that requires both strength in your upper body and core, and flexibility in your back. Take it at your own speed and only raise your feet as high as is comfortable. Over time, you'll be able to increase the lift higher.

- Start in a kneeling position.
- Bring your palms onto the floor with your fingers faced sideways on either side of your knees.
- Bend your arms and lean forward, putting the weight of your chest onto the backs of your upper arms and side of the head, creating a tripod.
- Kick one leg up at a time, coming into your Locust balance.

Leg Lifts

These extended lower body lifts are a terrific way to work stomach, side, and back muscles, as well as building core strength and improving spinal flexibility. Make sure to anchor yourself with pressure from your arms and hands.

284

One Legged King Pigeon Pose 1

Eka Pada Rajakapotasana is an advanced pose that stretches the hips, thighs, spine, chest, shoulders, neck, and abdominals and is especially good for strengthening the spine. Avoid this pose if you have any problems with or injuries to your hips, back, or knees. You can hold this pose from 10 seconds to 1 full minute.

Annotation Key
Bold text indicates strengthening muscles
Black text indicates stretching muscles
* indicates deep muscles

deltoideus medialis

coracobrachialis*

latissimus dorsi

serratus anterior

pectoralis minor*

pectoralis major

rectus abdominis

obliquus internus*

obliquus externus

transversus abdominis*

sartorius

quadratus lumborum

gluteus maximus

biceps femoris

gluteus medius

vastus lateralis   rectus femoris

iliopsoas*   vastus medialis

- Begin in Downward Facing Dog (#338). Bend your left leg and bring your left knee forward between your hands. Place your leg sideways on floor, still bent, with heel facing your pubis.
- Slide your right leg back, flat on the floor, your knee pointing down.
- Push down with your fingertips, raise your chest, and bring your torso upright. Tilt your head back and elevate your chin.
- Bend your right knee, flexing your foot so the sole is toward the crown of your head. Reach back with both hands, and grasp your toes from outside the foot. Return to an upright pose and reverse legs.

285 One Legged King Pigeon Pose 2

Begin with One Legged King Pigeon Pose 1 (#284). Then tilt your head upright as your left hand releases the left toes; place your left hand on your right knee. Take your right arm, cross it under your left arm and grasp the toes of the left foot, with the heel positioned close to your buttocks. Hold for 30 to 60 seconds, then switch arms and legs.

286 Easy One Legged King Pigeon Pose

While transitioning into One Legged King Pigeon Pose 1 (#284), tuck your left leg under your groin instead of pressing it to the floor. You can also leave the fingertips of one hand on the floor for balance. Remember to sit deep in this pose, drawing your groin toward the floor.

287 One Legged King Pigeon Pose 3

In this version of the pose, you will reach back to grasp your toes instead of reaching up.

- Begin in One Legged King Pigeon Pose 1 (#284).
- With your head upright, lean forward so that your chest is over your left knee.
- With elbow slightly bent, place your left palm on the floor.
- With your right elbow bent and your shoulder parallel to the floor, grasp the toes of your right foot and draw it toward your buttocks.
- Hold for 30 to 60 seconds; reverse to the opposite arm and leg.

288 One Legged King Pigeon Pose 4

In One Legged King Pigeon Pose 2 (#285), with your left hand holding the left leg, move your left hand to your right knee, still bent on the floor, and reach back with your right arm and grasp your left shin, midway between knee and ankle. Hold for 30 to 60 seconds, then switch to hold your right leg with your left arm.

289 Pose of the Heavenly Spirits Preparation

This pose requires a lot of flexibility in the spine as well as extension of the arms and shoulders. Make sure you have prepared for it by completing several basic back and shoulder poses beforehand.

- In One Legged Pigeon Pose 3 (#287), tilt your head back slightly.
- Reach back with both arms to your bent left leg and grasp it by the ankle.
- The lower leg should be perpendicular to the floor. Shift the position of the right foot if necessary for leverage.
- Hold for 15 to 30 seconds, then switch to the right leg and foot.

290 King Pigeon Arm Extended

While in One Legged King Pigeon Pose 1 (#284), with both hands holding the toes of your right leg, release your right hand from your toes and raise right arm straight overhead, fingers pointing up. Hold for 30 to 60 seconds, then switch to the right hand on your left foot, with your left arm in the air.

291 One Legged King Pigeon Pose Preparation

Sit upright with your right leg bent, your thigh and shin flat on the floor, heel toward the pubis, and your left leg straight back, knee pointed down. Place your right hand, palm up, on your right knee, your left hand on your left foot, palm up, and form Gyan Mudra with your fingers.

Head Up

In this pose, the head should remain upright and the neck in neutral position. The back should be relatively straight without a noticeable arch. Sit deep into the pose, drawing the groin to the floor.

292 One Legged King Pigeon Pose 5

While in basic One Legged King Pigeon Pose 1 (#284), unbend your right leg and extend it forward, toes pointed, and release your right hand, so that the left hand alone is grasping the toes of the left leg. Hold for 15 to 30 seconds, then switch to grasp your right toes with your right hand.

293 One Legged King Pigeon Pose 6

This pose stretches the thighs, abs, groin, shoulders, neck, and chest, and is thought to stimulate the abdominal organs. Be sure to keep your glutes, hamstrings, and pelvic floor fully engaged.

- While in One Legged King Pigeon Pose 1 (#284), holding your left toes with the right and left hands, straighten the right leg and extend it forward.
- Decrease the arch of your back, and raise your head so that your neck is in neutral position.

Lord of the Dance Pose 1

Natarajasana, known as Lord of the Dance Pose, is an advanced pose that requires foundation, stability, flexibility, and concentration. It stretches the shoulders, chest, abdominals, groin, and thighs, and strengthens the spine, thighs, hips, and ankles. It is also important for improving your sense of balance.

Correct form
Keep the bottom leg straight and contract your muscles during the pose. Brace your free hand on a wall if at first you have trouble maintaining balance.

Avoid
Do not look down at the floor while in pose, which can make you lose your balance. Don't compress the lower back.

Annotation Key
Bold text indicates strengthening muscles
Black text indicates stretching muscles
* indicates deep muscles

pectoralis minor

deltoideus anterior

pectoralis major

latissimus dorsi

serratus anterior

rectus abdominis

obliquus externus

obliquus internus*

quadratus lumborum

transversus abdominis*

iliopsoas*

sartorius

vastus medialis

tibialis anterior

gastrocnemius

vastus lateralis

rectus femoris

gluteus maximus

gluteus medius*

biceps femoris   semitendinosus

- In Mountain Pose (#001), bend your right knee and raise your right heel toward your buttocks, keeping the hips open.
- Reach your right hand back and grasp the inside of your right ankle.
- Lifting through your tailbone, spine, and neck, raise your right foot toward the ceiling. At the same time, raise your left arm toward the ceiling, forming Gyan Mudra. Hold for 20 to 60 seconds; repeat on the other side.

295 Lord of the Dance Preparation

Before attempting the Lord of the Dance pose, try this pose, which requires less elevation or extension in the raised leg.

Open Arms

While in this position, remember to keep your chest open and your arms wide. It might help to imagine that you are a temple dancer with raised arms playing finger cymbals as you concentrate on the muscles of your supporting leg.

- Begin by standing and raising your right foot with your knee bent and reaching back to grasp your toes with your right hand.
- Shift your toes to inside the elbow of your right arm—your elbow can be lowered slightly—and then raise both hands while forming Gyan Mudra.
- Hold for 30 to 60 seconds, then switch to raising the opposite leg.

296 Lord of the Dance Pose 2

In Lord of the Dance Pose 1 (#294)—left hand holding the inside of the left ankle—straighten your left leg upward. Extend your right arm, forming the Gyan Mudra with your right hand.

Regain Balance

While raising your back leg, it is normal for your torso to shift forward. Lifting your arm and chest will allow you to regain a more upright stance. It also increases your flexibility.

297

Lord of the Dance Foot to Elbow

While in Lord of the Dance Pose 2 (#296), with right leg raised, move your hand to outside of your foot and slide the foot toward the elbow of your right arm. Tilt your upper torso forward while maintaining balance. The left arm should be held out to the side.

- While in Lord of the Dance Foot to Elbow pose (#297), with your right foot tucked in your right elbow and torso angled forward, slowly bend your left knee and extend your left arm out before you and keep your elbow bent.
- With both hands form the Gyan Mudra.
- Hold for 20 to 30 seconds, then switch to the left foot in the left elbow.

298

Lord of the Dance Knee Bent

This pose does not require you to do a deep bend at the knee. When in proper position, your two thighs should almost form a straight line.

299 Lord of the Dance Hands to Foot

In this more difficult version of the pose, it helps to begin by consciously shifting the weight of the body to one foot as you raise the opposite leg and foot. As with the basic Lord of the Dance, this pose stretches the shoulders, chest, thighs, groin, and abdomen. It helps to strengthen the legs and ankles and is great for improving your sense of balance.

- In Mountain Pose (#001), bend your right knee and raise your right heel toward your buttocks.
- Reach back with your right hand, palm outward, and grasp your toes.
- Rotate your shoulder so that your right elbow points to the ceiling.
- Rotate your left hand back to grasp your right wrist. Walk the left hand up until both hands are grasping the right toes.
- Hold for 20 to 40 seconds; release the leg and repeat, using opposite leg.

Improve Your Reach
If at first you have trouble grasping the raised foot in these poses, try using a foot strap until your flexibility improves.

300 Bound Lord of the Dance Pose

In Lord of the Dance Hands to Foot pose (#299), holding your left foot, release your left arm and slide it behind your left thigh. Maintain the elevation of your left leg while holding your toes with the right hand. Hold for 20 to 30 seconds, then raise the other foot.

Opposite Sides
Like all poses that involve left arm/right leg, or right arm/left leg connections, this one works the muscles of the back, abdomen, and sides.

CHAPTER FOUR

Arm Routines

Many yoga poses include on-arm supports and inversions. Arm supports focus on the arms, shoulders, and chest, strengthening the abdominals and increasing spine and hip flexibility. They are also effective for reversing the age-related weakening of bones and muscles, and preventing osteoporosis. Inversion poses place the head below the heart—reversing gravity's effects on the body and benefiting the cardiovascular, lymphatic, nervous, and endocrine systems. They increase circulation and promote healthier lung tissue. When starting out, hold these poses for a short time only and pay attention to neck position.

301

Plank Pose

This beginner/intermediate pose—which has no agreed-upon Sanskrit name—strengthens and tones the arms, abdominals, and wrists. While in pose, it is important to distribute your weight evenly, so make sure to lengthen your legs down to your heels.

Correct form
Your body should form a straight line from head to heels. Squeeze buttocks and draw in abdominals for stability.

Avoid
Do not allow buttocks to poke up or hips to sag; don't sink or hunch your shoulders.

Annotation Key
Bold text indicates strengthening muscles
Black text indicates stretching muscles
* indicates deep muscles

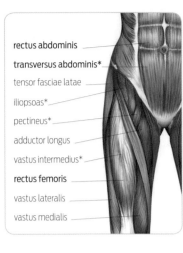

rectus abdominis
transversus abdominis*
tensor fasciae latae
iliopsoas*
pectineus*
adductor longus
vastus intermedius*
rectus femoris
vastus lateralis
vastus medialis

trapezius
teres minor
teres major
erector spinae*
piriformis
gluteus maximus
gluteus medius*
semitendinosus
deltoideus posterior
deltoideus anterior
triceps brachii
pectoralis major
serratus anterior
obliquus externus*
obliquus internus*
biceps femoris
semimembranosus
gastrocnemius

- Begin by kneeling upright, and shift forward so your upper torso is supported by your arms—the wrists below shoulders, palms flat on the floor.
- Extend your legs until you are resting on tiptoes.
- Broaden your shoulder blades, and engage your legs. Hold for 30 seconds to 1 minute.

302

Plank Pose Preparation
Begin by kneeling, leaning forward with your forearms perpendicular to the floor. Extend your legs straight back on tiptoes.

303 One Handed Extended Four Limbed Staff Pose

While in Plank Pose (#301), separate your feet slightly and then reach out with one arm, keeping it aligned with the angle of your torso.

304 One Legged Extended Four Limbed Staff Pose 1

This variation of the Plank Pose works the entire dorsal area, from neck to spine to buttocks, to thighs, hamstrings, and heels. Make sure to support your weight at both ends and keep the arch of your back high and domed.

· From basic Plank Pose (#301), angle your head down between your arms, while arching your back upward.

· Bring your right knee forward far enough to touch your face.

· Hold for 30 seconds to 1 minute, then repeat with the opposite leg.

305 One Legged Extended Four Limbed Staff Pose 2

From Plank Pose (#301), hook the left foot over the right calf so that it is just above the right ankle, sole facing outward.

306 One Legged Extended Four Limbed Staff Pose 3

While in basic Plank Pose (#301), raise the right leg, toes pointed and with the sole of the foot facing the ceiling; hold for 30 seconds to 1 minute. Repeat with the left leg.

307

Alternating Four Limbed Staff Pose

From Plank Pose (#301), raise your left leg parallel to the floor, toes pointing, and raise your right arm straight out from the shoulder, fingers pointing forward. Hold for 15 to 30 seconds, then raise the other leg and arm.

308

Staff Pose Revolved One Hand Extended

From Plank Pose (#301), lower your knees to floor, and raise your right arm straight up, fingers outstretched. While propped on your left arm, straighten both legs, feet together. Hold for 15 to 30 seconds, then reverse sides.

309

Staff Pose Dedicated to Makara

From Plank Pose (#301)— your legs and torso propped up on straight arms—lower your body to rest on your forearms, with your elbows positioned below your shoulders. Clasp both hands together.

310 One Hand Staff Pose

While in Staff Pose Dedicated to Makara (#309), with your palms down, swing your right arm straight out from your shoulder, then reach it forward and up, fingers spread. Hold for 30 seconds; reverse to the other arm.

311 One Leg Staff Pose

From Staff Pose Dedicated to Makara (#309), raise your right leg with toes pointed to align with the rest of your torso. Keep the neck in neutral position. Hold for 15 to 30 seconds, then raise the reverse leg.

312 Staff Pose Revolved One Hand

From Staff Pose Dedicated to Makara (#309), lower your knees to the floor, raise your right arm up toward the ceiling, with the palm flat—forming a straight line from your left elbow to right hand—and then straighten your legs.

313

Chaturanga

Also known as the Chaturanga Dandasana, the Four Limbed Staff Pose, or the Low Plank, this pose strengthens the abdominal muscles, the triceps, the pectorals, shoulder blades, and wrists. If you find the pose difficult at first, keep your knees on the floor. Do not attempt this pose if you have shoulder, wrist, or lower back injuries.

Correct form
Tighten your buttock muscles and tuck in your stomach muscles to maintain stability; keep your legs engaged and extended.

Avoid
Do not let your shoulders sink down or hunch up; remember to keep your neck in neutral position.

trapezius

deltoideus medialis

infraspinatus*

supraspinatus*

subscapularis*

teres major

rhomboideus*

Annotation Key
Bold text indicates strengthening muscles
Black text indicates stretching muscles
* indicates deep muscles

teres minor

triceps brachii

gluteus maximus

serratus anterior

pectoralis minor*

pectoralis major

- From Plank Pose (#301), open your chest and broaden your shoulders, while tucking in your tailbone.
- Exhale and turn in your legs slightly; lower yourself until your upper arms are parallel to your spine.
- Draw your abdominals in toward your spine and keep your elbows tucked in along your sides. Hold for 15 to 30 seconds.

Form a Line
Ideally, in this variation of the Plank Pose, your entire torso and legs should be arranged in a straight line and nearly parallel to the floor.

314 Four Limbed Staff Pose

From Chaturanga (#313), lower your knees to the floor and lower your chest until it is within 1 inch (2.5 cm) of the floor; hold for 15 to 30 seconds.

315 Revolved Four Limbed Staff Pose

From Chaturanga (#313), rotate your lower body, with legs straight and ankles together, until you are resting on your left side, keeping the shoulders squared. Repeat by rotating to the other side.

316 One Legged Four Limbed Staff Pose

From Chaturanga (#313), lower your chest almost to the floor; lift and straighten your right leg, keeping your toes pointed. Hold for 20 to 30 seconds; repeat with the left leg.

317 Staff Pose Leg to Side

From Chaturanga (#313), rotate your right leg at the hip to form a right angle with the body, sole facing outward. Try to keep the extended leg the same distance from the floor as your torso.

318 One Hand Four Limbed Staff Pose

From Chaturanga (#313), straighten your arms and angle your torso up; your spread feet shoulder-width apart. Bend the left arm and position the palm above your heart; hold for 15 to 30 seconds.

319

Side Plank

Vasisthasana, or Side Plank, is a beginner pose that strengthens the wrist, arms, legs, and abdominals, and is very good for improving your sense of balance. You should not attempt this pose if you have wrist or elbow injuries or issues with your shoulders.

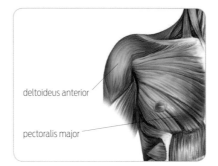

deltoideus anterior

pectoralis major

Annotation Key
Bold text indicates strengthening muscles
Black text indicates stretching muscles
* indicates deep muscles

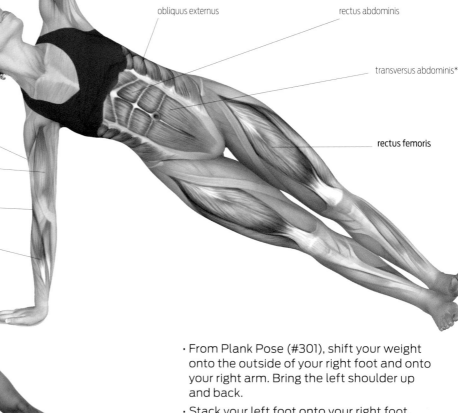

obliquus externus

rectus abdominis

transversus abdominis*

brachialis

biceps brachii

brachioradialis

flexor digitorum*

rectus femoris

- From Plank Pose (#301), shift your weight onto the outside of your right foot and onto your right arm. Bring the left shoulder up and back.

- Stack your left foot onto your right foot, squeezing your legs together while straightening them.

- Exhale, and raise your left arm up to the ceiling; gaze at your fingertips. Hold for 15 to 30 seconds; repeat on the other side.

320

Pose Dedicated to Sage Vasishta

From left Side Plank (#319), cross your right leg over the outstretched left leg, and place your foot on the floor. Drop your right arm along your body, then raise it toward the ceiling; gaze at your fingers.

321

Tree Pose in Pose Dedicated to Sage Vasishta

From left Side Plank (#319), bend your right leg and place your foot on the inside of the upper thigh, with your hand on the right knee. Tilt the supporting foot outward to raise the angle of your hips.

322

Revolved Leg to Side Pose Dedicated to Sage Vasishta

This variation of the Side Plank honors Sage Vasishta, who was a revered Vedic sage and author. Vasishta was famous in Hindu mythology as the owner of the divine cow Kamadhenu and her offspring Nandini, and for his conflicts with Sage Vishvamitra.

- From right Side Plank (#319), bend your right leg and bring your right foot to your left knee.
- Rest your left hand on your left knee, with your hand forming Gyan Mudra,
- Raise your left arm perpendicular to your torso, with your hand outstretched. Hold, then reverse sides.

323 One Big Toe Pose Dedicated to Sage Vasishta

From Side Plank (#319), bend the right knee, toes pointing back. Raise your left leg out from the hip, and grasp your left toe with your left hand. Alternatively, perform the toehold in full Side Plank.

324 Pose Dedicated to Sage Vishvamitra

This variation of the Side Plank honors Sage Vishvamitra, one of the most venerated sages of ancient India. He was also a king and a noted warrior, but he gave up his throne to gain spiritual power. This pose requires flexibility of the hips and core muscles and a well-developed sense of balance.

- From left Side Plank Pose (#319), rotate your left leg and position it behind your left arm, your foot facing up.
- With your right arm arched over your head, grasp the outer side of your left foot.
- Hold for 15 to 30 seconds; repeat with right foot.

325 Knee Plank to Side

From Side Plank (#319), rest on your left forearm; bring your knees to the floor with your lower legs angled back, feet together and off the floor. Raise your right arm toward the ceiling; gaze at your palm.

326 Side Plank Supported

From right Side Plank (#301), with your legs extended, place your left hand on your hip and lower your torso to rest on your right forearm. Hold for 15 to 30 seconds; reverse sides.

327 Side Plank Support with Arm Extended

While performing this variation of the basic Side Plank Pose, be sure to maintain your balance by engaging your core and buttock muscles to keep you stable.

- Begin in left Side Plank Supported (#326)— your legs extended, feet stacked, and your left arm raised to the ceiling.

- Bend your left leg over your right leg and place your foot on tiptoes just below the upper right thigh. Hold for 15 to 30 seconds; switch sides.

328 Side Plank Supported with Top Bent Knee

From left Side Plank Supported (#326), your right leg stacked on the left leg, and right arm raised, bend your right leg and place the outside of right foot, toes pointed, against the upper thigh. Hold for 15 to 30 seconds.

329

Crow Pose

Also called Crane Pose or Bakasana, this intermediate pose strengthens and tones the arms, shoulders, abdominals, and wrists. It is also an effective way to improve balance and is a good introductory pose to master balancing on your arms.

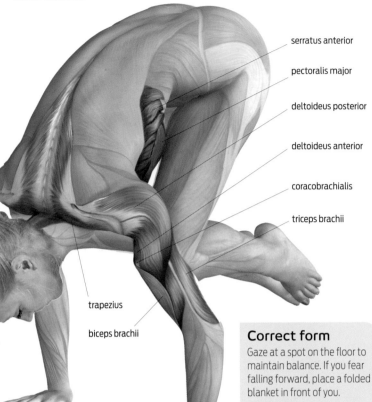

serratus anterior

pectoralis major

deltoideus posterior

deltoideus anterior

coracobrachialis

triceps brachii

trapezius

biceps brachii

iliopsoas*

Correct form
Gaze at a spot on the floor to maintain balance. If you fear falling forward, place a folded blanket in front of you.

Avoid
Do not "jump" into the posture—raise one foot at a time. Do not drop your head, but keep it in neutral position.

- Lower yourself into a deep squat, buttocks lower than your knees. Lean your torso forward and place your heads in front of you, fingers spread.
- Bend your elbows and rest your knees against your upper arms; boost your torso up on tiptoes and slide your shins along your upper arms.
- Shift your weight onto your wrists one foot at a time, tottering until you find your balance. Hold for 20 seconds to 1 minute.

330

Side Crow Pose 1
Crouch with your hands down, arms apart to the left of your bent knees. Place the outside of your left thigh on the upper part of your right arm; lean forward to lift your pelvis and thighs off the floor.

331 Eight Angle Pose

Crouch with your hands down, arms apart, and with your left arm behind your right knee. Lean forward to lift your pelvis and thighs off the floor. Cross your left foot over your right foot.

332 Rooster Pose

From Full Lotus Pose (#415), pass your hands past your calves and thighs and place them flat on the floor, your arms near your knees. Exhale; lift your body off the floor, supporting your weight on your wrists and hands.

333 Pendant Pose

Sit on your heels with your calves crossed, knees bent. Place both arms down at your hips, shoulder-width apart, and rock yourself up, lifting your torso forward off the floor, and shifting your legs behind you.

334 Crane Pose Knees off Triceps

From basic Crow Pose (#329), shift your weight—your center of gravity—forward until you can actually raise your knees slightly from your triceps, keeping your knees bent and your feet together, toes pointed.

335 Two Handed Arm Balance

From Crow Pose (#329), slowly lower your torso as you straighten your supporting arms and straighten both legs; spread them out to each side so that your inner thighs are against your upper arms.

336 One Legged Crow Pose

From Crow Pose (#329), shift your weight forward to bring your elbows under your chest and then extend your legs behind you, toes pointing. Bend your left knee and bring it up to your left tricep.

337 Side Crow Pose 2

From Side Crow Pose 1 (#330), with bent legs resting on a single elbow, raise your hips and angle your upper torso further forward.

338

Downward Facing Dog

Also called Adho Mukha Svanasana, this beginner pose stretches the shoulders, hamstrings, and calves, and strengthens the arms and legs. Avoid it if you have carpal tunnel syndrome.

gluteus maximus

latissimus dorsi

serratus anterior

deltoideus posterior

triceps brachii

semitendinosus

biceps femoris

gastrocnemius

- Kneel on your hands and knees, with your knees below the hips and your toes bent. Exhale and lift your sit bones toward the ceiling.
- Press your heels and palms to the floor as you straighten your knees and elbows, keeping your head between your arms. Hold for 30 seconds to 2 minutes.

Correct form
First practice this pose with knees bent and heels up. Contract your thighs to lengthen the spine and relieve pressure from the shoulders.

Avoid
Do not let your shoulders sink into your armpits; keep your spine from rounding.

339 Revolved Downward Dog
From Downward Facing Dog (#338), twist at the waist as you reach back with your right hand to touch the outer edge of your left foot.

340 Downward Dog Tiptoes
From Dogward Facing Dog (#338), arch your back up, rise on tiptoes, and bend your knees, bringing them forward to touch your forehead.

341 Downward Dog Wide Feet
From Downward Facing Dog (#338), spread your legs apart as wide as is comfortable with your soles down. Hold for 30 seconds to 1 minute.

342 Downward Dog Forehead to Ground

From Downward Facing Dog (#338), inch your arms carefully forward on your palms, keeping your feet planted, until you can rest your head on the mat.

343 Downward Dog Supported

From Downward Facing Dog (#338), inch your arms carefully forward on your palms, keeping your feet planted, until you can rest your head on the mat. Slide your arms back, bending your elbows until you can place your forearms on the mat and lift your head off the ground.

344 Downward Dog Hands Bound

Perform Downward Facing Dog (#338) with your legs spread. Inch your arms carefully forward on your palms, keeping your feet planted, until you can rest your head on the mat. Transfer your weight to your head, and raise your arms with hands Reverse Bound.

345 Shivalinga

From a kneeling position, fold down your torso and lower your head so that the top of your head rests on the floor, near your thighs. Bring both arms forward, parallel to floor, and clasp your hands.

346 Ear Pressure Pose

From Shivalinga (#345), bring your arms back to grasp the soles of your feet, drawing your head near or against your thighs.

347 Downward Dog with Bent Knee

From Downward Facing Dog (#338), raise your right leg until the thigh is parallel to floor, then bend your knee and point the toes. Make sure to keep your spine straight and your head down between your arms.

348 Downward Dog Leg Extension

While in Downward Facing Dog (#338), raise your right leg straight up, toes pointing toward the ceiling. Hold for 15 to 30 seconds, then switch legs.

Stay Grounded

In any raised, extended pose, it is important to maintain the position of the grounded, supporting arms and legs and to keep the spine and head in alignment.

349

Plow Pose

Also called the Halasana, this intermediate pose relieves stress, eases headaches and backaches, and stimulates digestion.

Annotation Key
Bold text indicates strengthening muscles
Black text indicates stretching muscles
* indicates deep muscles

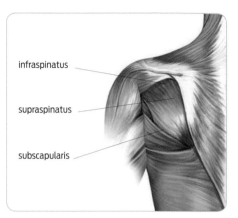

infraspinatus

supraspinatus

subscapularis

- Lie supine, arms at sides, then bend your knees and raise your legs off the floor, pressing with your arms to elevate your hips and buttocks.
- Roll your back up off the floor, supporting your lower back with bent arms.
- Extend your legs over your head, and lower toes to the floor.

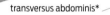

transversus abdominis*

triceps brachii

Correct form
Your torso should be nearly perpendicular to the floor. Soften your throat; relax the tongue. Place a folded blanket under the shoulders to ease your back.

Avoid
Don't swing your legs down into the pose; lower them gradually, with control.

350

Plow Modification
From Plow Pose (#349), with legs your extended and your toes curled forward on the floor, stretch your toes into a point as you bring legs closer to your head. Support the small of your back with your raised hands.

351 Plow
Bound Hands

This is a slightly advanced modification of the Plow Pose. Placing your hands in the Bound Position increases the stretch you will experience in your shoulders.

- Begin in Plow Pose (#349), with your arms shoulder-width apart and your torso perpendicular to the floor.
- Bring your hands together and clasp them.
- Hold for 30 seconds to 1 minute.

352 Plow Pose Hands to Toes

From Plow Modification pose (#350), reach above your shoulders with both arms and grasp your feet. Your hips will now be positioned beyond your shoulders.

353 One Legged Plow Pose

From Plow Pose (#349), bring your right arm beside your head, bent elbow up, and your hand on the floor. Rest the straightened right leg on your elbow, while bending your left leg.

354

Shoulder Stand

Also called Salamba Sarvangasana or Supported Shoulder Stand, this intermediate pose stretches the shoulders, neck, and upper spine, stimulates digestion, and is good for relieving stress. Practice near a wall and walk your feet up it if you can't lift your pelvis into the stand.

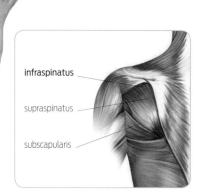

infraspinatus

supraspinatus

subscapularis

- Lie supine, arms at sides; bend your knees, pressing with your arms to elevate your hips and buttocks.
- Roll back up from floor, raising your legs up, and supporting your lower back with your hands.
- Hold for 30 seconds to 5 minutes.

Correct form
Soften your throat and relax your tongue. Place a folded blanket under your shoulders if the pose strains your neck.

Avoid
Do not bend your hips once you are in the pose—it puts pressure on your neck and spine; don't splay your elbows out to the sides.

Annotation Key
Bold text indicates strengthening muscles
Black text indicates stretching muscles
* indicates deep muscles

biceps femoris

gluteus maximus

gluteus medius*

latissimus dorsi

triceps brachii

transversus abdominis*

rectus abdominis

355

Inverted Shoulder Stand
While in Shoulder Stand (#354)—legs elevated, toes pointed—reach forward with your right leg until your foot is on the floor, your toes facing your head. Hold for 30 seconds to 1 minute, then reverse legs.

356 Shoulder Stand Supported One Leg

From Shoulder Stand (#354), bring your left leg forward, toes pointed, to rest on the floor. Hold for 30 seconds to 1 minute; then reverse legs.

357 Leg Contraction Pose

From Shoulder Stand (#354), bend your left knee and bring it even with hip, toes pointed to ceiling. Hold for 30 seconds to 1 minute; then reverse legs.

358 Shoulder Stand Hands Bound

From Shoulder Stand (#354), find your center of gravity as you remove your hands from supporting your back; extend them behind you with your hands clasped.

359 Shoulder Stand Unsupported Hand to Calf

From Shoulder Stand (#354), bring your right leg down to touch the floor and grasp the calf with both hands. The elevated leg will come forward.

360 Extended Hand to Toe Pose in Shoulder Stand

From Shoulder Stand (#354), lower your left leg to touch the floor and grasp your toes with your left hand. Place your right arm behind you for support.

361 Leg Position of Pose Dedicated to Garuda

From Shoulder Stand (#354), bend your left leg slightly and wrap your right calf over your left knee. Keep your spine perpendicular to the floor.

362 One Legged Unsupported Whole Body Pose

From Shoulder Stand (#354), lower your right leg so that your toes are on the floor facing you as you raise both hands to your thighs.

363 Shoulder Stand Unsupported Pose

From Shoulder Stand (#354), angle your torso and legs a bit more over your head, and raise your arms up until your hands are flat on your thighs.

364

Head Stand

The Salamba Sirsasana is an advanced pose that strengthens and tones the abdominals, and strengthens the arms, legs, and spine. It is especially good for improving balance. If you cannot keep your spine from sagging or rounding during the leg elevation, bend your knees slightly.

Correct form
Your torso should be perpendicular to the floor before you extend your legs up. If you can't balance during the headstand, practice with the back of your shoulders against a wall.

Annotation Key
Bold text indicates
strengthening muscles
Black text indicates
stretching muscles
* indicates deep muscles

Avoid
Don't put too much weight on your neck; distribute it evenly on your forearms. Don't jump into the pose or kick up one foot at a time.

- From Downward Dog Forehead to Ground (#342), cradle your head in your arms with interlaced fingers.
- Walk your legs forward as you shift your weight to your shoulders and forearms until your sit bones face the ceiling. Exhale, bend your knees, with your toes up, and draw your thighs to your abdomen. Breathe and find your balance.
- Exhale, and slowly lift your toes toward the ceiling—extending your legs and tucking your tailbone toward the pubis. Hold for 10 seconds to 3 minutes.
- Release the pose by lowering both feet simultaneously.

gluteus medius*

transversus abdominis*

rectus abdominis

trapezius

latissimus dorsi

deltoideus medialis

triceps brachii

365

One Legged Head Stand
From Head Stand (#364), with both legs straight up, toes pointed to ceiling, shift your right leg back slightly, and bring your left leg forward from the hip, with the toes nearly touching the floor.

366 Leg Contraction Knee Bend Pose

From basic Head Stand (#364), your legs elevated, shift your right leg back slightly and bring your left leg forward, bending your knee so that the thigh is parallel to the floor, and the toes are pointing to the ceiling.

367 Svastika Legs

This challenging variation of the Head Stand requires control, concentration, and great core stability. The Svastika, or hooked cross, is an ancient and sacred Indian symbol meaning "good fortune" or "well-being." It may represent the movement of the sun through the sky.

- From basic Head Stand (#364), slowly separate both legs, with your thighs almost parallel to the floor.
- Bend forward the front leg, toes angled up, then bend the rear leg, toes angled down.

368 Seated Angle Pose

From basic Head Stand (#364), with weight on your forearms, slowly bend your knees outward until you can touch the soles of your feet together.

369 Upward Lotus Pose

From Head Stand (#364), move your legs into Lotus Pose by bending both knees outward, tucking your left heel back against your right buttock, placing your left calf against the right shin. Hold for 30 seconds to 2 minutes; reverse legs.

370 Crane Pose

From basic Head Stand (#364), separate your hands and place your palms flat on the floor. Bend your knees and bring your thighs down to touch your abdomen, with your lower leg and toes pointing up.

371 Crane Pose One Leg Extended

From Crane Pose (#370), with your knees bent and tucked against the abdomen, straighten your left leg out to the side, toes pointed. Hold for 30 seconds to 2 minutes, then reverse legs.

Upward Facing Plank

Annotation Key
Bold text indicates strengthening muscles
Black text indicates stretching muscles
* indicates deep muscles

The Purvottanasana is an intermediate pose that strengthens the spine, arms, and hamstrings as well as extending the hips and chest. Remember to breathe steadily, using your breath to deepen the extension of your back. Do not attempt this pose if you have neck or wrist injuries.

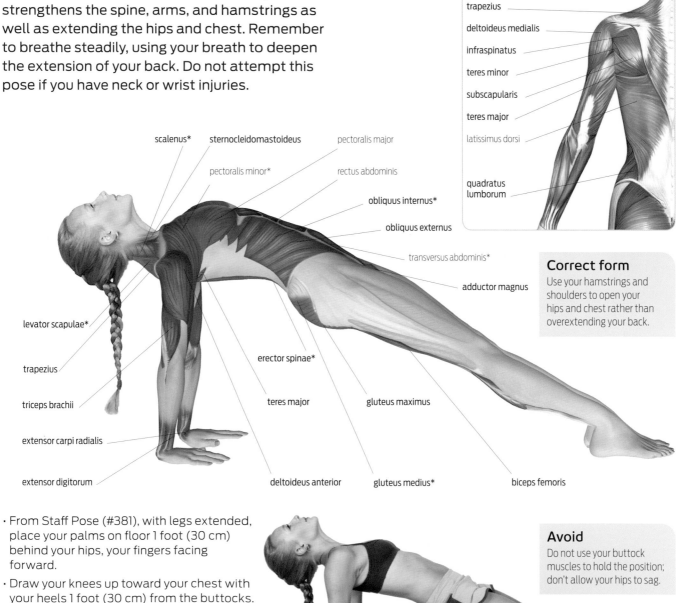

trapezius
deltoideus medialis
infraspinatus
teres minor
subscapularis
teres major
latissimus dorsi
quadratus lumborum

scalenus*
sternocleidomastoideus
pectoralis major
pectoralis minor*
rectus abdominis
obliquus internus*
obliquus externus
transversus abdominis*
adductor magnus
levator scapulae*
trapezius
triceps brachii
extensor carpi radialis
extensor digitorum
erector spinae*
teres major
gluteus maximus
deltoideus anterior
gluteus medius*
biceps femoris

Correct form
Use your hamstrings and shoulders to open your hips and chest rather than overextending your back.

- From Staff Pose (#381), with legs extended, place your palms on floor 1 foot (30 cm) behind your hips, your fingers facing forward.
- Draw your knees up toward your chest with your heels 1 foot (30 cm) from the buttocks.
- Lift your hips until your back and thighs are parallel to the floor. Straighten your legs one at a time. Lift your chest and bring the shoulder blades together to create an arch in your back. Elongate your neck and let it drop back. Hold for 30 seconds.

Avoid
Do not use your buttock muscles to hold the position; don't allow your hips to sag.

373 Feet Wide Eastern Intense Stretch

This variation of the Upward Facing Plank requires even more extension of the lower legs and places emphasis on the hamstrings. Make sure to keep your shoulder blades together to open your chest. If your hamstrings are too weak to hold the lift at first, bend your knees slightly.

Heel relief
This may be a helpful pose for those who suffer from plantar fasciitis—it stretches both the heels and the calves.

- Begin in Upward Facing Plank (#372), with your legs extended, feet together, and toes pointing forward.
- Shift your legs until they are shoulder-width apart, and raise your feet up until your weight is on your heels with your toes pointing to the ceiling.
- Hold for 30 seconds before returning to Staff Pose (#381).

374 Eastern Intense Stretch Pose
From Upward Facing Plank (#372), lower yourself onto your elbows, raise your toes up slightly, and form a shallow arch with your legs, buttocks, spine, and shoulders.

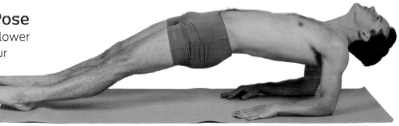

375 Half Eastern Intense Stretch Pose
From Upward Facing Plank (#372)—arms and legs straight—bend your knees and dip your buttocks down toward the floor. Make sure to keep your upper body and head in the same position, your back slightly arched up.

376 Tiptoe Half Eastern Intense Stretch Pose

This variation of the Upward Facing Plank engages the tips of the fingers and the toes, making it a useful pose for improving stability, concentration, and balance. Make sure to keep your chin up and your neck elongated as your head tilts back; don't crunch your neck into your shoulders.

- From Upward Facing Plank (#372), your arms and legs extended and your hips elevated, bend your knees and lower your buttocks so they are about 1 foot (30 cm) from the floor.
- Raise yourself up onto your toes and your fingertips. Your spine should remain fairly straight, not arched.
- Hold for 15 to 30 seconds, then return to Staff Pose.

377 One Legged Half Eastern Intense Stretch Pose 1

Lie supine with your arms outstretched, palms down. Shift your lower torso onto one hip; tuck your left foot and calf under the right knee. Hold for 30 seconds to 1 minute, then reverse legs.

378 One Legged Half Eastern Intense Stretch Pose 2

From One Legged Half Eastern Intense Stretch Pose 1 (#377), bring your right hand down to your left knee and press your knee gently to the floor.

379 One Legged on Forearm

From Upward Facing Plank (#372), bend your left knee and left elbow, so you are resting on your left forearm. Raise your right leg and place your right foot on your left knee. Raise your right arm and bring your hand to your right ear.

380 Revolved Hand to Foot Pose in Half Eastern Intense Stretch Pose

This is another variation of Upward Facing Plank that will help you to improve balance, control, and concentration. Make sure that your weight is evenly distributed between the supporting forearm and foot and that you keep your neck elongated.

· From Upward Facing Plank (#372), ease down onto your right elbow.

· Bend your left knee so that it is at a right angle to the floor, the sole flat.

· Extend your right leg straight up from the hip, your toes pointing to the ceiling.

· Raise your left arm and grasp the outer ankle of your right leg.

CHAPTER FIVE

Seated Poses & Twists

Seated yoga poses, or asanas, strengthen the core and improve posture and spinal flexibility. Performing seated asanas relieves tension along the spine and provides a relaxing and grounding experience. Generally, we meditate in seated asanas that help to align the chakras from the base of the spine to the crown of the head.

Seated yoga twists promote a greater range of motion along the spine and alleviate back pain. Twisting asanas energize the body by lengthening the spine and opening the spaces between the vertebrae. Add some twists to your yoga sequences as a refreshing counterpoint to forward bends and backbends.

381

Staff Pose

Staff Pose, also known as Stick Pose and Dandasana, is a grounding position that helps to improve posture. Visualize the spine as the "staff" that connects the crown of the head to the bottom of the tailbone.

Correct form
Rotate your thighs slightly inward, and push out through your heels as you flex your feet. Push your shoulder blades down.

Avoid
Don't curve your back; place a rolled towel under your hips if needed to correct your position.

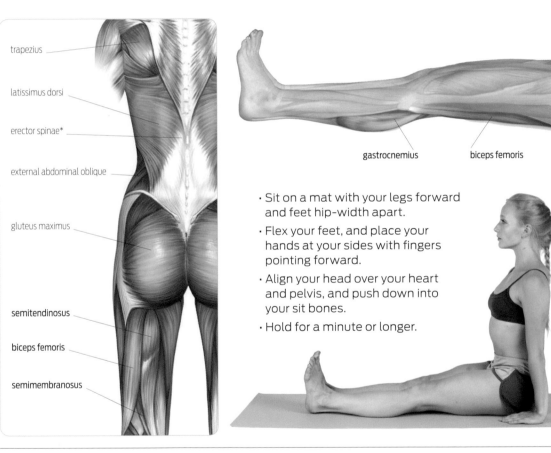

gastrocnemius   biceps femoris

trapezius

latissimus dorsi

erector spinae*

external abdominal oblique

gluteus maximus

semitendinosus

biceps femoris

semimembranosus

- Sit on a mat with your legs forward and feet hip-width apart.
- Flex your feet, and place your hands at your sides with fingers pointing forward.
- Align your head over your heart and pelvis, and push down into your sit bones.
- Hold for a minute or longer.

382   Reverse Prayer Staff Pose

Begin in Staff Pose. Roll your shoulders back, and reach your hands behind your back. Press your palms together in Reverse Prayer Position between your shoulder blades. Draw your shoulders down and elbows back.

383 Staff Pose Heart to Sky 1

Begin in Staff Pose (#381). Place your palms flat on the mat behind you, fingers pointing forward. Roll your shoulders back, and open your chest. Turn your gaze upward and hold for a minute.

384 Staff Pose Heart to Sky 2

Begin in Staff Pose (#381). Place your palms flat on the mat behind you, fingers pointing away from your torso. Roll your shoulders back, lean your head back, and open your chest. Turn your gaze upward.

385 Staff Pose Revolved

Begin in Staff Pose (#381) and reach your arms overhead. Twist your torso to the left. Press your right hand onto your left knee, and place your left hand behind you. Shift your gaze over your shoulder.

386 Staff Pose Revolved with Arm Extended

Adding a twist to this Staff Pose variation opens the shoulders and chest. It also increases flexibility in the hips and pelvis while stretching the obliques.

- Begin in Staff Pose (#381) and raise your arms overhead.
- Twist to your left, and reach your right hand to the outside of your left ankle.
- Extend your left arm up behind you, and gaze over your left shoulder.

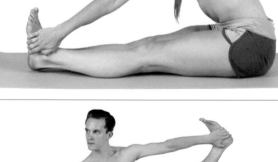

387 Staff Pose Revolved, Hand to Ankle

Begin in Staff Pose (#381). Twist your torso to the right, and place your right hand behind you. Bend your right knee, reach your left hand to your right ankle, and straighten the raised leg.

388

Easy Pose

Easy Pose, also known as Sukhasana or Pleasant Pose, is a common asana for meditation. This calming pose is a good alternative to the Lotus Pose if your hips are tight. Easy Pose helps open the hips and outer thighs. In Sukhasana, your legs should be loosely crossed, so when you look down, your thighs should form a triangle with your shins.

Annotation Key
Bold text indicates strengthening muscles
Black text indicates stretching muscles
* indicates deep muscles

rectus abdominis
transversus abdominis*

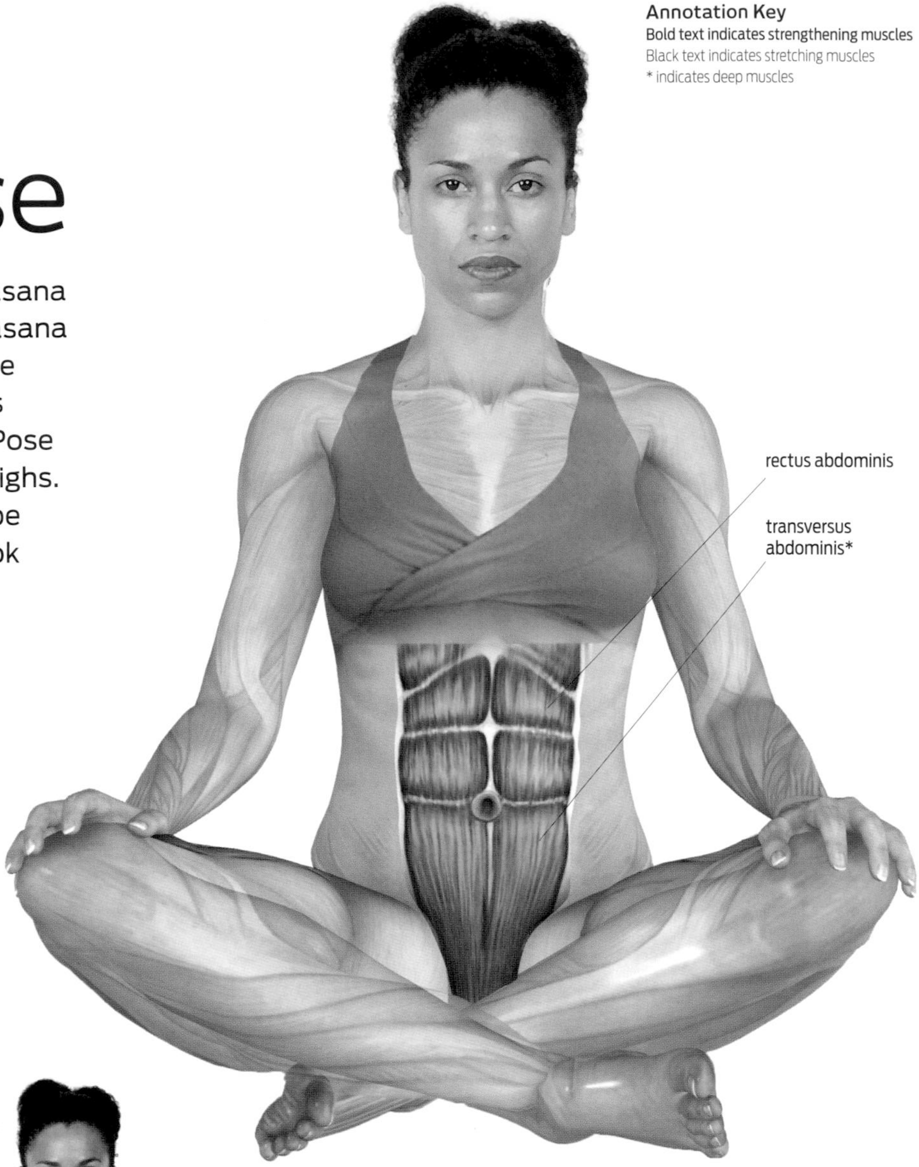

Correct form

Your hips should be above your knees. If your hips are very tight, place a folded blanket under your hips for support.

Avoid

Don't always cross the same leg over the other; alternate leg positions. Avoid tucking your shins too close to your body.

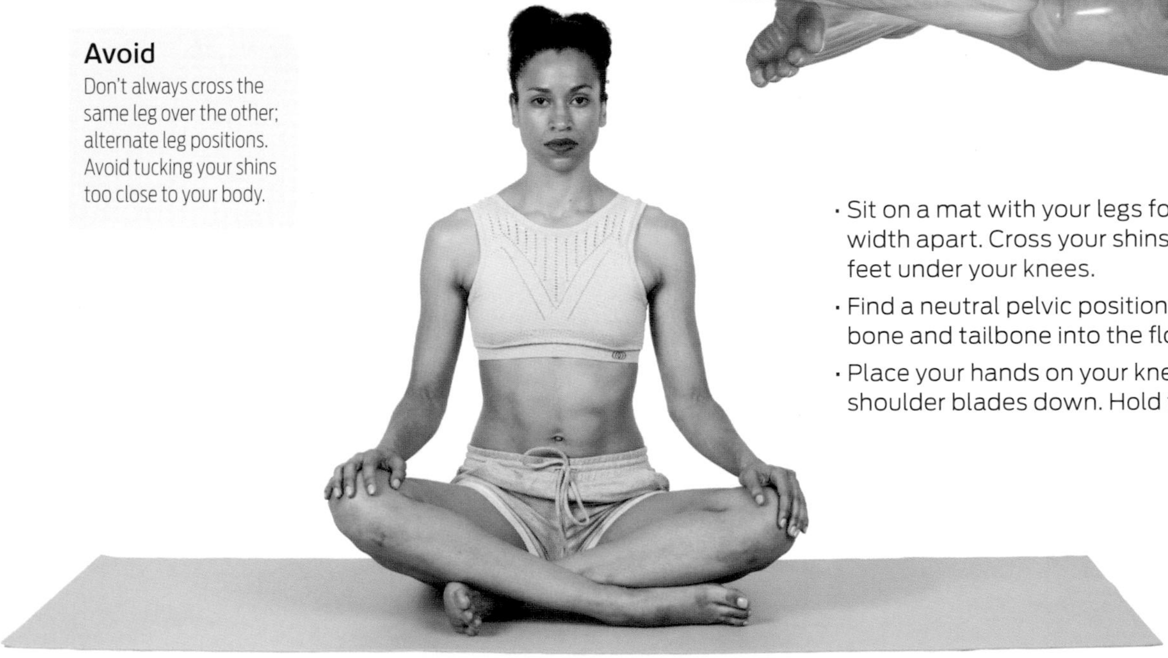

- Sit on a mat with your legs forward and about hip-width apart. Cross your shins loosely and tuck your feet under your knees.
- Find a neutral pelvic position and press your pubic bone and tailbone into the floor.
- Place your hands on your knees and push your shoulder blades down. Hold for 1 minute.

389 Easy Pose Knees to Chest

Begin in Easy Pose (#388), then raise your knees toward your chest. Place your elbows on your knees and rest your face in your palms.

390 Easy Pose on Block

Prepare in Easy Pose (#388), except support your hips on a yoga block. Rest your hands on your knees, palms up. Touch your thumb and index finger together in the Gyan Mudra, or gesture of consciousness.

391 Easy Pose Revolved

Prepare in Easy Pose (#388). Place your right hand behind you, and your left hand on your right knee. Twist to your right, keeping your chest open and your head aligned with your spine and tailbone.

392 Sideways Easy Pose

Begin in Easy Pose (#388), and reach your left arm overhead with your fingers in Gyan Mudra. Bend to your right, and place your right forearm on the mat at your side. Open your chest and gaze upward.

393 Easy Pose Embryo in Womb

Begin in Easy Pose (#388), and wrap each hand around the opposite ankle. Balance on your sit bones and hold for several breaths.

394 Accomplished Pose

Begin in Easy Pose (#388). Tuck one foot between the opposite thigh and calf. Place your hands on your knees, and form the Gyan Mudra. Place your palms down for a grounding feeling, or palms up to connect with the divine.

395

Hero Pose

The calming Hero Pose, or Virasana, is an excellent position for meditation. It appears simple but requires a fair amount of flexibility in your knees. To perform this pose safely, be sure to use your yoga props. If your knees are uncomfortable, place a yoga block between your feet for support. A folded blanket or two under your shins will ease any discomfort in your ankles.

Correct form
Sit tall and keep your back in neutral position. Push your shoulder blades down while lengthening your tailbone into the mat. Your thighs should be touching and rotated slightly inward. The tops of your feet should be flat on the floor.

Avoid
Don't hunch your shoulders or pop out your ribcage. Avoid straining your knees or ankles.

Annotation Key
Bold text indicates strengthening muscles
Black text indicates stretching muscles
* indicates deep muscles

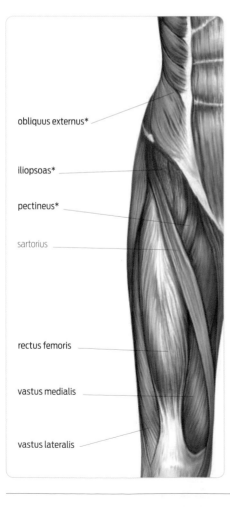

obliquus externus*

iliopsoas*

pectineus*

sartorius

rectus femoris

vastus medialis

vastus lateralis

extensor hallucis

tensor fasciae latae

- Kneel on the mat with your knees close together and feet slightly more than hip-width apart.
- Position the tops of your feet flat on the floor and point your toes behind you.
- Lower your hips to the mat so your heels are touching your outer hips.
- Hold for several deep breaths.

396 Tiptoe Hero Pose

Kneel on a mat, with your knees and feet together. Lower your hips onto your heels. Lengthen your spine, keeping your back in neutral position. Press your palms together and bring your hands to your heart in the Anjali Mudra. Gaze forward and hold for 1 minute.

397 Tiptoe Hero Arms Extended

Tiptoe Hero Arms Extended strengthens your core while stretching your arms and chest. As you reach your arms upward, feel the energy release through your fingertips.

- Kneel on all fours, with your knees and feet about hip-width apart.
- Gaze downward as you lower your hips onto your heels.
- Press your shoulders down and your shoulder blades together as you raise your arms out to your sides.
- Touch your thumbs and index fingers together in Gyan Mudra and hold for 1 minute.

Mudras and the Mind

Mudras are spiritual hand gestures that stimulate the flow of prana, or energy, through the body. Each finger represents a specific emotion. The outward expression of a Mudra is an affirmation of the mind-body connection.

398 Hero Pose Cat Tilt Forward Bend

Kneel on a mat, or a folded blanket, with legs pressed together. Bend forward at the waist, curling your head and back. Rest your hands on your knees and hold for 1 minute.

399 Hero Pose Dog Tilt Backbend

Kneel on a mat, or a folded blanket, with your legs together. Rest your hands on your knees. Arch your back as you turn your gaze upward. Lengthen your spine and hold for 1 minute.

400 Hero Pose Raised Bound Hands

Kneel on a mat, or a folded blanket, with your legs parallel. Clasp your hands together in front of you, and press your palms outward. Inhale, and extend your arms toward the ceiling.

401 Hero Scale Pose

The Hero Scale Pose is an advanced stretch for your ankles and the tops of your feet. For a simpler version of this pose, keep the tops of your feet and ankles on the mat, and place your hands on the floor behind you.

- Kneel on a mat with your feet about hip-width apart. Lower your hips onto your heels and curl in your tailbone.
- Walk your hands behind you, and lift your knees off the mat.
- Engage your abdominals, and reach your arms around your knees.
- Hold for a few breaths and gently release.

402 Hero Pose Heart Opener

Begin in Hero Pose (#395), and cross your arms behind you. Press your shoulders down as you turn your face upward, stretching your chest, neck, and shoulders. Hold each foot with the opposite hand.

Heart-Opening Poses

Heart openers stretch your chest and ribcage and help to energize your body and soothe your soul. Visualize opening your heart as you perform back-extending poses.

403 Hero Pose Revolved

Prepare as in Hero Pose (#395), and twist to your right. Place your right hand on the mat behind you, and your left hand near your right thigh. Turn your gaze to your right and lengthen your spine. Hold for 1 minute.

404 Hero Pose, Knees Wide

Kneel on a mat, with your knees wide apart and toes together. Lower your hips onto your heels. Lengthen your spine and feel the stretch in your inner thighs.

405

Cow Face Pose

Cow Face Pose, or Gomukhasana, deeply stretches the shoulders and back, and opens the hip flexors and knees. Don't see the resemblance to a cow's face? Imagine that the legs are the cow's mouth, the torso is the cow's nose, and the arms are the cow's ears.

Correct form
Distribute your weight evenly across your sit bones. For proper balance, be sure to raise the elbow on the same side of your body as the bottom knee.

Annotation Key
Bold text indicates strengthening muscles
Black text indicates stretching muscles
* indicates deep muscles

triceps brachii

deltoideus medialis

latissimus dorsi

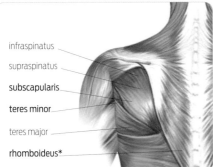

infraspinatus
supraspinatus
subscapularis
teres minor
teres major
rhomboideus*

Avoid
Don't curl your shoulders forward or collapse your chest; instead, open your chest and collarbones.

- Begin in Staff Pose (#381) with your legs forward. Bend your knees, and cross your left leg over your right, stacking your knees.
- Rest the sides of your feet on the mat.
- Pull your shoulder blades down and lengthen your spine as you inhale and reach your right hand to the back of your neck.
- Exhale, reach your left hand behind your back, and attempt to clasp your hands together.
- Hold for 30 seconds and alternate sides.

Cow Face with Ganesha Mudra

Begin in Staff Pose (#381). Bend your knees and cross your left leg over your right. Raise your elbows out to the sides, and bring your left hand to your heart. Clasp your fingers together in the Ganesha Mudra to lift your spirits.

Cow Face Hands to Feet

Begin in Staff Pose (#381). Bend your knees and cross your right leg over your left, tucking your feet into your hips. Open your chest and cross your arms behind you, reaching each hand to the opposite foot.

408 Cow Face Arms Overhead

If the arm position of Cow Face is too difficult, try this easier modification with arms crossed overhead. Another simple variation is to hold a towel or strap behind your back.

- Begin in Staff Pose (#381). Bend your knees and cross your right leg over your left, stacking your knees.
- Rest the sides of your feet on the mat. Pull your shoulder blades down and lengthen your spine.
- Cross your arms overhead and shift your gaze down to your knees. Hold for 1 minute.

409 Cow Face Prayer Hands

Begin in Staff Pose (#381) with legs forward. Bend your knees and cross your right leg over your left, stacking your knees. Press your palms together near your heart in the Anjali Mudra (Prayer Hands), and bow your head.

410 Cow Face Forward Bend

Cow Face Forward Bend variation deeply stretches the hips and lower back while lengthening the arms. Hip-openers such as this pose release the negative energy that we tend to store in our pelvic area.

- Begin in Staff Pose (#381). Bend your knees and cross your right leg over your left, stacking your knees.
- Hinge your hips forward and lean your torso into your thighs.
- Extend your arms out to the sides, touching the floor with your fingertips, and gaze forward.

411 Cow Face Side Bend

Begin in Staff Pose (#381) with legs forward. Stack your right knee over your left. Bend your torso to the right, and reach your right hand to your left foot. Extend your left hand overhead and toward the ceiling. Hold for 1 minute and alternate sides.

412 Revolved Cow Face Side Bend

Revolved Cow Face Side Bend stretches your spine, hips, and shoulders. This variation also stimulates the internal organs. Gaze upward to open your chest and heart, and feel the energy release from your fingertips.

- Begin in Staff Pose (#381). Stack your left knee over your right.
- Lengthen your spine, pulling your shoulders down, and extend your right arm across your left thigh.
- Reach your left arm overhead, and turn your gaze toward the ceiling.
- Form the Gyan Mudra, by bringing the thumbs and index fingers together.

Twisted Poses

Revolved poses, or twists, massage your abdominal muscles and your organs. Twists improve your digestion and circulation, expelling toxins from your body.

413 Revolved Cow Face Pose

Begin in Staff Pose (#381). Stack your left knee over your right. Lengthen your spine, and twist to your left. Cross your right arm in front of you, resting your hand on your waist. Extend your right hand behind you to touch your left foot.

414 Cow Face Balance

Begin in Staff Pose (#381). Stack your right knee over your left. Wrap your hands around your ankles and shift your weight to the back of your sit bones. Raise your legs from the mat, and extend your elbows out to your sides.

415

Full Lotus Pose

Full Lotus Pose, or Padmasana, is an excellent position for meditation and for yoga in general. Lotus provides a sense of stability and grounding, but it requires a considerable degree of flexibility in the hips, knees, and ankles. To prepare for Full Lotus Pose, first practice Half Lotus Pose. You should be able to hold Half Lotus for several breaths comfortably before attempting Full Lotus.

Annotation Key
Bold text indicates strengthening muscles
Black text indicates stretching muscles
* indicates deep muscles

transversus abdominis*

tibialis anterior

rectus abdominis

obliquus externus

- Begin in Easy Pose (#388), with your legs loosely crossed.
- Lift your right shin, and place your right foot on your left thigh. Hold this Half Lotus for a breath.
- Lift your left shin, and place your left foot on your right thigh.
- Tuck your heels in close to your torso, and position your feet so the soles face upward.

416 Half Lotus Pose

Begin in Easy Pose (#388) with your legs loosely crossed. Lift your left shin, and place your leftfoot on your right thigh. Tuck your heel in close to your torso with the sole facing upward. Form the Gyan Mudra with your thumbs and index fingers.

417 Lotus Pose Reverse Prayer

Begin in Full Lotus Pose (#415). Reach your hands behind your back, and bring your palms together in Prayer Position. Keep your shoulders down, and press your shoulder blades together.

418 Lotus Pose Bound

Begin in Full Lotus Pose (#415). Keep your shoulders down and press your shoulder blades together, as you cross your arms behind your back. Touch each hand to the opposite thigh.

Why The Lotus Blossom?

The lotus flower is a metaphor for grounding oneself in the earth to achieve enlightenment. The lotus has deep roots in the mud and grows on a long stem in the water before it can reach sunlight and blossom.

419 Lotus with Backward-Bound Hands

Begin in Easy Pose (#388) with your legs loosely crossed. Lift your right shin, and place your foot on your left thigh. Lift your left shin, and position your left foot on your right thigh. Tuck in your heels, and position your feet with soles facing upward. Extend your arms behind your back, and clasp your hands together. Turn your gaze toward the ceiling.

The Seventh Chakra: Wisdom

A "1,000-petaled" lotus flower symbolizes the seventh chakra, Sahasrara, at the crown of the head. It represents a higher consciousness and a spiritual connection to the world.

420 Lotus with Palms to Ground

Begin in Full Lotus Pose (#415). Place your palms flat on the floor behind your back, with fingers pointing toward your hips. Open your heart as you press your shoulder blades together. Turn your gaze toward the ceiling.

421 Lotus with Upward-Bound Hands

Incorporate a shoulder stretch into your Lotus Pose for a full-body workout. Lengthen your spine, and open your chest as you reach your hands toward the ceiling.

- Begin in Full Lotus Pose (#415).
- Clasp your hands together, and press your palms outward.
- Reach your hands toward the ceiling.
- Turn your gaze upward and hold for 1 minute.

422 Lotus Forward Bend

Begin in Full Lotus Pose (#415). Clasp your hands together, inhale, and press your palms toward the ceiling. Lean forward from your hips, and extend your arms forward on the floor in front of you.

423 Revolved Lotus Pose

Begin in Full Lotus Pose (#415). Clasp your hands together, inhale, and press your palms together in the Anjali Mudra, or Prayer Hands. Exhale, and twist your torso to the right, touching your left elbow to your right knee.

424 Lotus Thread the Needle

Lotus Thread the Needle provides a deep spinal stretch and provides relief from back pain. If you're comfortable in this advanced position, perform circles with your raised arm to improve flexibility in your shoulders.

- Begin in Full Lotus Pose (#415), and place your hands on the floor in front of you.
- Thread your left arm between your right arm and your torso.
- Rest your arm flat on the floor and perpendicular to your torso.
- Turn your head toward the right, and extend your right arm overhead. Hold for several breaths.

425 Lotus Bound Hands Forward Bend

Begin in Full Lotus Pose (#415). Clasp your hands behind your back, and lean forward from your hips. Extend your clasped hands toward the ceiling.

426

Boat Pose

Boat Pose demands strength as you balance on the tripod of sit bones and tailbone. Paripurna Navasana targets your abdominals, lower back, and deep hip flexors. If you have difficulty straightening your knees, try using a strap around the soles of your feet to assist you.

Correct form
Push your shoulder blades down your back. Find your balance between your sit bones and your tailbone. Press your inner thighs together, rotating them slightly inward.

Avoid
Don't arch your back or pop out your ribcage. Avoid tensing your neck and jawline; tilt your chin slightly in toward your chest to loosen any tension.

vastus lateralis

rectus femoris

biceps femoris

triceps brachii

vastus intermedius*

rectus abdominis

iliopsoas*

obliquus externus

transversus abdominis

Annotation Key
Bold text indicates strengthening muscles
Black text indicates stretching muscles
* indicates deep muscles

- Sit in Staff Pose (#381) with your legs forward and hands at your sides.
- Bend your knees and lift your feet, so your shins are parallel to the floor.
- Engage your abs and extend your arms forward and parallel to the floor.
- Lean back slightly, and extend your legs and arms to 45 degrees. Hold for 30 seconds if possible.

427 Easy Boat Pose 1

Sit in Staff Pose (#381) with your legs forward and hands at your sides. Bend your knees and lift your feet, so your shins are parallel to the floor. Wrap your arms behind your thighs, and lean back slightly.

428 Easy Boat Pose 2

Sit in Staff Pose (#381) with your legs forward and hands at your sides. Bend your knees and lift your feet, so your shins are parallel to the floor. Engage your abs, and reach your hands to the outsides of your feet. Lean back slightly, and hold for 30 seconds or longer.

429 Supported Boat Pose 1

This simple modification, Supported Boat Pose 1, is appropriate for those who have the flexibility to straighten their legs but lack the strength to maintain the Full Boat Pose.

- Begin in Staff Pose (#381) with your legs forward.
- Place your hands behind you, fingers pointing forward.
- Bend your knees and lift your feet, so your shins are parallel to the floor.
- Lean back slightly, bending your elbows, and extend your legs to 45 degrees.

430 Supported Boat Pose 2

Sit in Staff Pose (#381) with your legs forward and hands at your sides. Bend your knees and lift your feet, so your shins are parallel to the floor. Clasp your hands behind your thighs. Lean back slightly, and hold for 30 seconds or longer.

431 Half Boat Pose

Lie on the floor with your knees bent, and clasp your hands behind your head. Extend your feet to 45 degrees from the floor, and curl your upper back from the mat. Hold for 30 seconds.

The Third Chakra: Warrior Energy

Manipura, the fire chakra, resides in the navel area and is the seat of self-confidence and warrior energy.

432 Revolved Boat Pose with Prayer Hands

Boat Pose with the Anjali Mudra adds a sense of peace and unity: Pressing the palms together unifies the right and left sides of the brain, and pressing the thumbs to the chest opens the heart.

- Begin in Staff Pose (#381), with legs forward and hands at your sides.
- Bend your knees and lift your feet, so your shins are parallel to the floor.
- Lean back slightly, and press your palms together at your chest.
- Twist your torso to the left, and turn your gaze upward.

433 Revolved Boat Pose Supported

Begin in Staff Pose (#381). Bend your knees, and cross your right foot over your left. Place your right hand on your ankle, lift your legs, and straighten them to 45 degrees. Lean back, twist your torso to the left, and place your left hand behind you.

434 Revolved Boat Pose

Sit in Staff Pose (#381). Bend your knees, and cross your right foot over your left. Lift your legs, and straighten them to 45 degrees. Place your hands on the floor at your sides.

435 Double Compass Pose

The advanced Double Compass Pose is a demanding pose that requires a great degree of balance, flexibility, and coordination. This pose stretches the hamstrings and spine, and stimulates the internal organs.

- Sit with knees bent, feet off the mat, and shins parallel to the floor.
- Extend your arms forward, and cross your left hand over your right.
- Hold each ankle with the opposite hand.
- Straighten your right arm and left leg.
- Pull the left elbow back, straighten the right leg, and bring the right knee to the right shoulder.

436 Big Toes Pose

Sit with knees bent. Lean back slightly and lift your legs, so your shins are parallel to the floor. Reach between your legs, and grab your big toes with either hand. Find your balance, and straighten your legs.

437

Sage Marichi's Pose 1

In Hindu mythology, Sage Marichi was the grandfather of the sun god, and in Sanskrit, Marichi means "ray of light." The powerful Marichyasana is an energizing twist that stretches the spine and calms the mind and spirit.

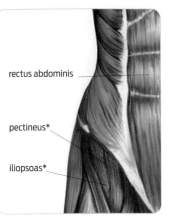

rectus abdominis

pectineus*

iliopsoas*

Annotation Key
Bold text indicates strengthening muscles
Black text indicates stretching muscles
* indicates deep muscles

obliquus externus*

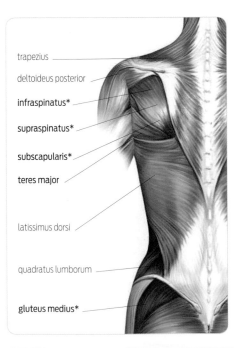

trapezius
deltoideus posterior
infraspinatus*
supraspinatus*
subscapularis*
teres major
latissimus dorsi
quadratus lumborum
gluteus medius*

Avoid
Don't let your extended foot twist outward; keep your foot flexed upward.

- Sit on a mat with your legs forward. Bend your left knee, and bring your heel in close to your torso.
- Press your right leg into the mat, rotating it slightly inward.
- Place your left hand behind you, fingers pointing away.
- Rotate to your left, and place your right elbow on the outside of your left knee.
- Turn your gaze to the left. Repeat on the opposite side.

438 Sage Marichi Preparation 1

Sit on a mat with your legs forward. Bend your right knee, and bring your heel in close to your torso. Lean forward, and wrap your hands around your extended foot.

439 Sage Marichi Preparation 2

Sit with your legs forward and feet flexed. Bend your left knee, and bring your heel in close to your torso. Extend your arms forward, parallel to the floor.

440 Sage Marichi's Pose 2

Prepare as in Sage Marichi Pose 1 (#437). Twist to the right, wrapping your left elbow around your right thigh. Reach your right arm behind your back, clasping your hands together.

441 Sage Marichi Supported Hand to Ankle

Sit on a mat with knees bent. Lean back on your right forearm, and grasp the outside of your right ankle with your left hand. Straighten your right leg.

442 Half Lord of the Fishes Marichi Twist

Sit on a mat with your legs forward. Bend your left knee, and cross your left foot over your right thigh. Place your right hand at your side, and reach for your right ankle with your left hand.

443 Half Lord of the Fishes Marichi Twist Supported

Sit on a mat with your legs forward. Bend your left knee and cross your left foot over your right thigh. Place your right forearm on the floor at your side, and reach for your right ankle with your left hand.

444 Spinal Twist

Sit on a mat with your legs forward. Bend your right knee, and cross your right foot over your left thigh. Place your left hand on the floor at your side, and touch your right hand to your left knee.

445 Bound Half Spinal Twist

Sit on a mat with your legs forward. Bend your right knee, and place your right foot on the floor by your left knee. Twist to the right and weave your left hand under your right knee. Press your palms together in Prayer Hands.

Monkey Pose

Monkey Pose, or Hanumanasana, is an advanced yoga pose that requires flexibility in the hip flexors and hamstrings. The name comes from the mythological monkey god, Hanuman, who leapt courageously across India to help his king. The message behind the legend is that power stems from devotion.

Correct form
Press your front heel and the top of your back foot into the floor. For support, use yoga blocks under your hands and the extended thigh.

Avoid
Don't overstretch; stop at a comfortable point and feel the stretch. Avoid rotating your hips or legs to the side.

Annotation Key
Bold text indicates strengthening muscles
Black text indicates stretching muscles
* indicates deep muscles

pectineus

adductor longus

vastus intermedius*

rectus femoris

tensor fasciae latae

gluteus maximus

semitendinosus

biceps femoris

vastus medialis

iliopsoas

vastus lateralis

· Kneel on the floor. Step your right foot forward into a low lunge.

· Lean slightly forward, and rest your fingertips on the floor at your sides for balance. Remain in this stretch for a few breaths.

· Slowly slide your right heel forward, straightening your leg. Descend only so far as you are comfortable. Reach your arms overhead and hold.

· To release, place your hands on the floor, bend your right leg outward, and slide your heel toward you.

447 **King Pigeon Pose Preparation**
Kneel on the floor. Lower your hips as you slide your right leg behind you. Place your hands on your hips, rotate your shoulders back, and open your heart to the sky.

448 **Monkey Pose Prayer Hands**
Perform as in Monkey Pose (#446), except press your palms together in Anjali Mudra. Touch your thumbs to your heart and hold for several breaths.

449 **Hanumanasana Backbend**
Perform as in Monkey Pose (#446). Press your palms together and extend your arms overhead and behind you. Open your heart to the sky.

450 **Hanumanasana Forward Bend**
Begin as in Monkey Pose (#446). Clasp your hands behind you and bend forward, touching your chin to your shin. Extend your arms toward the ceiling.

451 **Revolved Hanumanasana**
Begin as in Monkey Pose (#446), and twist your torso to the right. Place your hands on the opposite thighs and hold for several breaths.

452 **Revolved Hanumanasana Side Bend**
Begin as in Monkey Pose (#446). Twist your torso to the left and rest your right shoulder on your right knee. Extend your right arm along the side of your body. Reach your left hand overhead and touch your right toes.

453 **Revolved King Pigeon Preparation**
Begin as in Monkey Pose (#446). Twist your torso to the right, and with your right hand grasp your right foot and lift and bend it toward your torso. Repeat on the other side.

454 **One Knee Bent King Pigeon Pose**
Begin as in Monkey Pose (#446), and bend your left knee. Reach your left hand overhead and behind you to grab your raised toes. Extend your right arm toward the ceiling and form the Gyan Mudra.

455

Revolved Head to Knee Pose

Revolved Head to Knee Pose is a Twisting Pose combined with a Forward Bend. Parivrtta Janu Sirsasana stretches the side of the body, the diaphragm, and the intercostals. If at first the stretch is too difficult, begin by reaching for the shin of the extended leg instead of the foot.

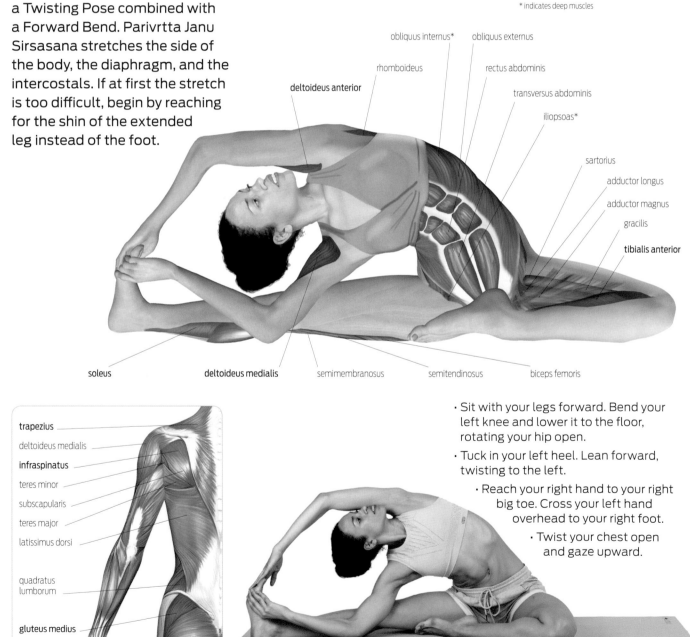

Correct form

Press the thigh of the bent leg into the floor to anchor yourself to the floor. Push your elbows away from each other to help twist your body.

Avoid

Don't release the pose by coming straight up from the revolved position; untwist your torso first, then return to upright.

Annotation Key
Bold text indicates strengthening muscles
Black text indicates stretching muscles
* indicates deep muscles

obliquus internus*
obliquus externus
rhomboideus
rectus abdominis
deltoideus anterior
transversus abdominis
iliopsoas*
sartorius
adductor longus
adductor magnus
gracilis
tibialis anterior

soleus
deltoideus medialis
semimembranosus
semitendinosus
biceps femoris

trapezius
deltoideus medialis
infraspinatus
teres minor
subscapularis
teres major
latissimus dorsi
quadratus lumborum
gluteus medius

- Sit with your legs forward. Bend your left knee and lower it to the floor, rotating your hip open.
- Tuck in your left heel. Lean forward, twisting to the left.
- Reach your right hand to your right big toe. Cross your left hand overhead to your right foot.
- Twist your chest open and gaze upward.

456 Seated Half Bound Half Hero Pose

Sit with your feet forward. Bend your left knee, and tuck your left foot close to your hip. Twist your torso to the left and place your right hand on your left knee. Reach your left hand behind your back, and touch your right hip. Twist your torso further and gaze over your shoulder.

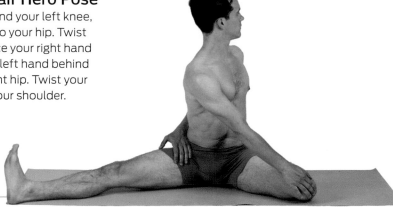

457 Seated Gate Pose

The Seated Gate Pose, or Parighasana, opens the chest and shoulders. It also stretches the spine and hip flexors and relieves tension in the neck and shoulders.

- Begin the exercise as in Revolved Head to Knee Pose (#455), except place your right hand on the floor near your right ankle.
- Flex your right foot.
- Twist your torso open to the left and reach your left arm overhead.
- Form the Gyan Mudra, with thumb and index finger.

458 Head to Knee Gate Preparation 1

Sit with your legs forward. Bend your right knee and lower it to the floor, rotating your hip open. Tuck your right heel into your left thigh, and flex your left foot. Lean forward, and reach your hands to your left ankle. Gaze forward and hold for 1 minute.

459 Head to Knee Gate Preparation 2

Sit with your legs forward. Bend your right knee and lower it to the floor, rotating your hip open. Tuck your heel into your left thigh. Lean forward, and reach your hands to your left ankle.

460 Head to Knee Pose

Head to Knee Pose, or Janu Sirsasana, is an energizing pose that increases flexibility in the spine, hamstrings, and shoulders. This exercise relieves tension and anxiety.

- Sit with your legs forward.
- Bend your left knee and lower it to the floor, rotating your hip open.
- Tuck your heel into your right thigh.
- Lean forward, and wrap your hands around your right ankle.
- Lower your forehead to your knee. Hold for 1 minute and repeat on the opposite leg.

461 Seated Half Bound Twist

Sit with your legs forward. Bend your left knee and lower it to the floor, rotating your hip open. Tuck your heel into your right thigh. Twist to your left, and place your right hand on your left knee. Reach your left hand behind your back, and touch your right hip.

462 Revolved Head to Knee Preparation

Sit with your legs forward. Bend your left knee and lower it to the floor, rotating your hip open. Tuck your heel into your right thigh. Lean to your right, and extend your right hand to your right toes.

463 Revolved Pose

Begin with Revolved Head to Knee Preparation (#462). Lean to your right, and reach your right hands to your right toes. Extend your left hand overhead. Turn your gaze upward and hold for 1 minute.

Side Bends

Side-bending poses open up the lungs and the intercostal muscles around the ribcage. These side stretches may help to alleviate lung conditions such as cold and asthma.

464 Seated Gate Stretch

Sit with your legs forward. Bend your left knee and lower it to the floor, rotating your hip open. Tuck your heel into your right thigh. Rest your right forearm along your inner right leg. Place your left hand behind you, and turn your gaze upward.

465 Seated Gate Pose with Bent Elbows

Seated Gate Pose with Bent Elbows engages the abdominals and stretches the shoulders, hips, and hamstrings. Try to bend from your hips rather than from your waist.

- Sit with your legs forward.
- Bend your left knee and lower it to the floor. Tuck your heel into your right thigh.
- Clasp your hands behind your head, and bend your torso to your right.
- Try to reach your right elbow to your right knee.
- Hold for 1 minute and repeat on the opposite leg.

CHAPTER SIX
Reclining Poses

Reclining poses serve several purposes. They offer a safe way to work leg and abdominal muscles with the hips and back supported by the ground, helping to avoid risk of injury. They also include warm-up poses—which are meant to awaken your muscles, increase your heart rate, and release tension; and cool-down poses—which lower the heart rate, relax muscles, and provide relief after a taxing workout. Knee to Chest Pose, which provides a counterpoint to backbends, is one example of a cool-down pose; Corpse Pose is another.

Reclining Poses

466

Reclining Twist

This beginner's pose enables you to release tension in the spine, loosen the hips, and tone the abdominal muscles. Make sure to start with your neck in neutral position. The pose should not be attempted by anyone with shoulder issues.

Correct form
Relax into the stretch; keep your chest open and elongate your spine. Try turning your head to both sides to alter the sensation.

Avoid
Don't tense your shoulders up to your ears or allow your shoulder blades to lift from the floor.

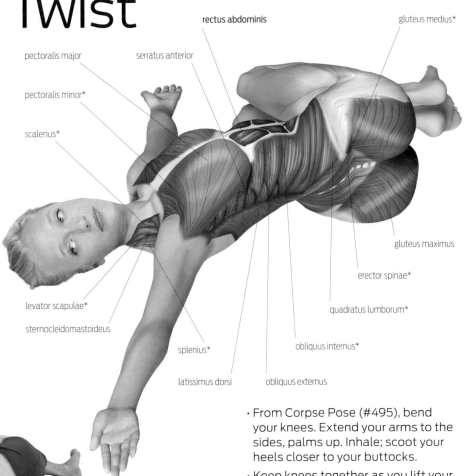

pectoralis major
rectus abdominis
serratus anterior
gluteus medius*
pectoralis minor*
scalenus*
gluteus maximus
erector spinae*
levator scapulae*
quadratus lumborum*
sternocleidomastoideus
splenius*
obliquus internus*
latissimus dorsi
obliquus externus

- From Corpse Pose (#495), bend your knees. Extend your arms to the sides, palms up. Inhale; scoot your heels closer to your buttocks.
- Keep knees together as you lift your legs from the floor. Exhale and angle both knees to the left while twisting hips and spine. Ease your left thigh to the floor as you gaze to the right.
- Hold for 30 seconds to 3 minutes; repeat on the opposite side.

467

Revolved Universal All-Encompassing Diamond Pose

From left-side Reclining Twist Pose (#466)—with your left thigh flat on the floor—bring your right knee up to your left hand, and then bring your left foot behind you to your right hand. Place the right sole on your left knee. Keep your shoulders flat on the floor. Hold for 30 seconds to 1 minute; then reverse legs.

468 Revolved Reclining Hand to Foot Pose

From right-side Reclining Twist (#466), gazing up, straighten both legs; then bring topmost left leg toward your right hand. Grasp the inner edge of your foot with your right hand.

469 Reclining Lord of the Fishes Pose 1

From left-side Reclining Twist (#466)—with the left thigh flat on the floor—straighten your left leg; then place your right knee flat on floor, with toes extended, and grasp it with your left hand.

470 Reclining Lord of the Fishes Pose 2

In a slight modification of the Reclining Lord of the Fishes Pose 1 (#469), place your hand on your thigh near your knee and draw your leg up so that your left shin is parallel to your right thigh.

471 Reclining Waist Pose

From right-side Reclining Twist (#466)—with your left thigh on floor—gradually straighten and shift both legs until they are angled up near your outstretched left hand, feet flexed. Hold for 15 to 30 seconds; repeat on the other side.

472 Sideways Reclining Angle Pose

From left-facing Reclining Waist Pose (#471), grasp your right foot by the big toe, then raise your left leg straight up from the hip, toes pointing to the ceiling. For added stretch, turn your head to the left.

473 Reclining Leg Position of the Half Cow Face

From right-facing Reclining Twist (#466), bring your left leg over your right knee, and plant your foot flat; assume Gyan Mudra, right hand on left knee, left hand on brow. Shift onto your right shoulder; extend right leg forward; raise flexed left foot, and wrap arms around throat. Recline back, legs again crossed over, and grasp the insteps of both feet.

474 Sideways Reclining Leg Position of the Pose Dedicated to Garuda

From right-facing Reclining Twist (#466), lengthen your right leg without straightening the knee, then bring left leg over right leg, and slide left calf under right knee. Hold for 30 seconds to 1 minute, then switch sides.

475

Knees to Chest Pose

Also called Apanasana, this beginner pose is beneficial for stretching the lower back and the hips. It is also useful for stimulating digestion. Do not perform this pose if you are pregnant or have recently had knee surgery.

gluteus medius*
piriformis*
obturator externus*
obturator internus*
adductor magnus
biceps femoris

Annotation Key
Bold text indicates
strengthening muscles
Black text indicates
stretching muscles
* indicates deep muscles

gluteus maximus

latissimus dorsi

- Lie supine on the floor. Exhale, and draw your bent knees up until your shins are parallel to the floor.
- Place your hands around the front of your knees. Lengthen the back of your neck away from your shoulders. With each exhalation, gently pull your knees closer to your chest as you flatten your back and shoulders on floor.
- Hold for 30 seconds to 1 minute.

Correct form
Make sure to keep your neck in neutral position. For a more challenging variation, wrap your arms around your knees and grasp the opposite elbow with each hand.

Avoid
While holding this pose, try not to tense your back or leg muscles.

476 Wind Relieving Pose

From Knees to Chest Pose (#475), slide your hands to your shins and draw your bent knees to your chest while rolling your hips and buttocks off the floor. This pose is effective for easing the cramping and pain of intestinal gas.

477 Reclining Waist Pose Preparation

From Knees to Chest Pose (#475), spread your arms wide from the shoulders and, keeping your knees together, place your left thigh flat on the floor. The thighs should be at a right angle to the torso. Hold for 30 seconds to 1 minute, then switch to the other side.

478 One Legged Wind Relieving Pose

From Knees to Chest Pose (#475), lower your left leg, toes pointed, and extend it out while drawing your bent right leg closer to your chest. This is another pose that helps to relieve intestinal gas pains and cramping.

479 Reclining Tree Pose

From Knees to Chest Pose (#475), extend your left leg straight out while lowering your right knee toward the floor. Use your right hand on your right knee to gently coax it to touch the floor.

Open Your Joints

In this pose, your hip and leg muscles need extension for your right knee to touch the mat. Don't ever force a limb into a pose; instead, focus on poses that improve flexibility.

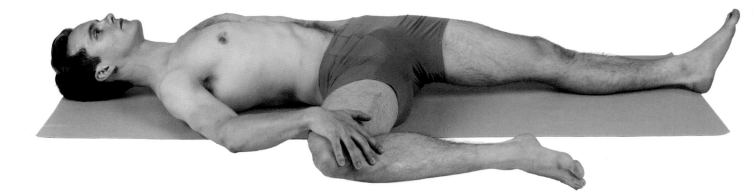

480 Reclining One Hand to Foot Pose

From Knees to Chest Pose (#475)—with both knees elevated—straighten out and lower your left leg, with foot flexed, toes up. Shift your right knee outside your right arm and reach up to grasp your heel with both hands.

Going Up

As you elevate your right leg, your left knee may bend slightly to compensate for your right buttock being raised up from the mat. Don't try to force that knee back to the floor.

481 Happy Baby Pose

Ananda Balasana provides a gentle stretch to the hips, inner groin, and lower back. It also elongates and aligns the spine and strengthens the arms and shoulders.

- Lie on your back; bring your knees to your chest and separate your knees and legs widely, holding onto each of your big toes.
- Raise your ankles above your knees, and gently draw your knees closer to your armpits.
- Lengthen your tailbone toward the mat and draw your shoulders onto your back, finding the natural curve of the lower back. Hold for 15 seconds to 1 minute.

482 Reclined Star Pose

From Knees to Chest Pose (#475), press your soles together, grasp both feet, and gently bring your toes forward to touch your forehead. Consciously round your spine as you raise your hips, buttocks, and lower back from the floor.

Get Loose

This pose, which requires flexibility of the back, hips, and legs, may take time to work up to. It makes a fine counterpoint to backbend poses, offering release to the back muscles.

483

Reclining Big Toe Pose 1

Also known as Supta Padangusthasana, this is one of the easier yoga poses, and it is practiced around the world. This pose strengthens the knee and stretches the hip, thigh, hamstring, and groin. Do not attempt this pose if you have had recent knee or hip surgery.

vastus medialis

gracilis*

biceps femoris

semitendinosus

vastus lateralis

gluteus maximus

transversus abdominis*

tensor fasciae latae

iliopsoas*

pectineus*

adductor magnus

adductor longus

Annotation Key
Bold text indicates strengthening muscles
Black text indicates stretching muscles
* indicates deep muscles

Correct form
Only straighten your leg enough that you can feel the stretch primarily in your hamstrings.

Avoid
Do not raise your buttocks from the mat—keep your hips firmly grounded; keep your neck elongated.

- Lie supine and raise your right leg over your torso, rotating the right thigh slightly so your knee faces your armpit.
- Grab the right big toe with the first and second fingers of your right hand. Keep your left hand clasping your left thigh. Use a foot strap if you can't grasp your toes.
- Hold for 15 to 30 seconds; repeat with the opposite limbs.

484 Reclining Big Toe Pose 2

From Knees to Chest Pose (#475), straighten your left leg and bring your right leg out to the side, at a 45-degree angle from your torso. Reach down with your right hand and grasp the big toe of your extended right leg.

485 Reclined One Legged Thunderbolt Pose

This variation of the Reclining Big Toe Pose (#475) allows the use of resistance bands (or a long towel) to really extend the stretch you achieve.

- Lie supine with your left foreleg on the ground, foot facing backward beside your hip.
- Raise your right leg slightly and toss the loop of a resistance band over your instep.
- Gently tug your leg to a 45-degree angle from the ground. Hold for 15 seconds to 1 minute, then repeat with the opposite leg.

486 Reclining Hands to Leg Pose 1

Lie supine, with knees bent, and soles pressed flat to the floor. Wrap both hands around the back of your right thigh and elevate your leg, with the bent knee positioned over your chest, foot arched, and toes pointing to the ceiling.

487

Reclining Half One Leg Extended Pose

Lie supine on the floor with your arms relaxed at your sides, knees bent, and heels drawn up close to your buttocks. Press your palms to the floor as you raise and straighten your right leg, toes angled up to the ceiling. Repeat on the other side

488

Reclining Hands to Leg Pose 2

Lie supine on the floor with your knees bent, and feet flat on the floor. Raise your left leg up over your torso until your stretched toes are above your head. Reach up with both hands and grasp your right ankle. Hold for 15 to 30 seconds, then repeat with the right leg.

489

Reclining Hands to Leg Pose 3

While in Reclining Hands to Leg Pose 2 (#488), bring your raised leg more upright and slide your hands down to clasp your calf. Remember not to roll your shoulders up off the mat as you reach.

Feel the Burn

You should definitely feel tension along the backs of your legs with this variation. Keep your knee as straight as possible to achieve the utmost benefit from the pose.

490

Reclining One Leg Extended Pose 1

From Reclining Big Toe Pose (#483), relax both arms at your sides, raising and extending your right leg straight overhead with the toes pointed to the ceiling. Keep your left leg extended on the floor with the toes pointing upward.

491 Reclining Big Toe Pose 3

From Reclining Big Toe Pose (#483), roll your right hip and buttock up while elevating your head and shoulders from the floor. Bring your forehead to your right shin, while grasping the toes of your right foot with your right hand.

492 Reclining Hands to Leg Pose 4

From Reclining Big Toe Pose 3 (#491), with left leg elevated and your right leg straight, point your right toes forward, and stretch your elevated left foot forward, toes pointed, as you grasp your left ankle with both hands.

493 Reclining One Hand to Leg Pose

From Reclining Big Toe Pose (#483)—right leg on the ground, foot flexed—raise your right arm, with your right hand on the outer ankle, to bring your left shin to your forehead. Use your left arm, palm flat, to aid balance and give you support.

494 Reclining One Leg Extended Pose 2

From Reclining One Hand to Leg Pose (#493)—left leg extended, foot flexed—keep the elevated right knee close to your forehead as you extend your flexed right foot and reach forward beside your hips with both arms, palms flat.

495

Corpse Pose

Also called Savasana, this beginner pose can calm the brain, relieve stress, and relax the body. It makes an ideal cool down after an intense session. Do not perform Corpse with a back injury.

Correct form
Pay attention to head alignment—pull your head away from your shoulders; do not tilt it. Practice this pose with your knees bent and feet flat on the floor.

Avoid
Try not to move once your body is in alignment. Do not tense your muscles.

- Lie supine with your arms a short distance from your body.
- Spread your shoulders and collarbone so that your palms face up and your fingers curl naturally.
- Spread your feet a comfortable distance apart, toes angled outward.
- Relax as you close your eyes and focus on aligning your body and breathing evenly.

Reclining Lotus Pose
From Corpse Pose (#495), position your legs in Lotus Pose—left foot tucked against the upper right thigh, right foot tucked into the bend of the left knee. Recline with your back slightly arched, and stretch your arms directly above your head, palms up.

Reclining Legs Extended Pose 1
From Corpse Pose (#495), raise both legs straight up from your hips, toes pointing to the ceiling. Cross your arms above your chest, wrists elevated even with your knees, and form the Gyan Mudra with the fingers of both hands.

498 Reclining Legs Extended Pose 2

From basic Corpse Pose (#495), raise both of your legs straight up, ankles together, without noticeably arching your back up from the floor; keep your toes pointed to the ceiling. Reach your arms straight up from your shoulders, with your fingers pointed to the ceiling. When in the correct pose, your body should form the letter U.

499 Half Upward Facing Intense Stretch

From Corpse Pose (#495), raise both legs and angle them over your torso so that your feet are above your head; grasp the back of your upper calves with both hands; hold for 30 seconds to 1 minute.

500 Upward Facing Western Intense Stretch

From Half Upward Facing Intense Stretch (#499), roll your buttocks and hips up from the floor and round your lower back. At the same time, slide your hands to your feet and grasp the insteps as you ease your shins down toward your face.

501 Reclined Hero Pose

This reclined pose, Supta Virasana, is especially good for opening up the hips and stretching the muscles of the knees, thighs, ankles, and abdomen.

- Sit, kneeling, with your calves on the outer side of your thighs, soles up.
- Ease your torso back, keeping your spine arched upward.
- Once your shoulders are grounded, reach back with both arms, palms up.
- Hold for 30 seconds to 1 minute.

Index of Exercises

Credits

Photography

Naila Ruechel

Photography Assistant

Finn Moore

Models

Natasha Diamond-Walker
Jessica Gambellur
Lloyd Knight
Daniel Wright

Additional Photography

Page 7 Bychykhin Olexandr/Shutterstock.com
Page 9 palawat744/Shutterstock.com
Pages 12–13 kudla/Shutterstock.com
Pages 44–45 May_Chanikran/Shutterstock.com
Pages 76–77 zhu difeng/Shutterstock.com
Pages 118–119 DR Travel Photo and Video/Shutterstock.com
Pages 144–145 Olga Danylenko/Shutterstock.com
Pages 174–175 Yuttana Jaowattana/Shutterstock.com

Illustration

All anatomical illustrations by Hector Diaz/3DLabz Animation Limited
Full-body anatomy and Insets by Linda Bucklin/Shutterstock.com